Yasuta  bu

of t
To
of

Pre-publi
REVIEW.
COMME
EVALUAT

This book helps readers to make sense of behavior that might otherwise seem confusing, contradictory, or downright illogical, and ensure that their business deals are not needlessly wrecked on the rocks of misinterpretation."

Peter J. Williamson, PhD
Visiting Professor
of International Business,
Harvard Business School

"**A**mong the many works that attempt to explain the way Japanese businesses work, this book stands out. It delves below the superficial differences to reveal the underlying values that drive Japanese businesspeople's thoughts and actions. It is an insider's view–written by a Japanese who also knows Western business.

Refreshingly, Sai not only presents the successful side of Japanese business values, but also flags the contradictions and presents some of the shortcomings that are inevitable in any business culture. The book also avoids the trap of simplistic stereotyping; it doesn't pretend for a moment that all Japanese businesspeople are exactly alike. Equally important, it addresses the issue of the new generation, and separates the things that are changing from the deeply rooted values that will endure as Japan continues to internationalize.

"**T**hrough his many years of studying Japanese management practices, Mr. Sai has developed a keen insight into the mind and motivation of the Japanese businessman. In defining the eight core values, he allows us an insight into how Japanese think and what drives them toward success. This book is useful for any Western businessperson who deals with the Japanese, or anyone who wants to gain a better understanding of the Japanese."

Paul Devermann
President, International Trade
and Transactions, San Diego

More pre-publication
REVIEWS, COMMENTARIES, EVALUATIONS . . .

"**T**he Eight Core Values of the Japanese Businessman fills a gap in transnational management literature. Mr. Sai identifies those 'core values' from his rich professional experience in Japan and many other countries, and as president of the know-how pool of the Japan Management Association. Interested readers will not only get revealing insights into Japanese management practice but also learn about human potential that could be mobilized.

The distinguishable Japanese paradigms, the values of Japanese managers, and the role of Japanese co-workers as co-thinkers in their enterprises are very clearly presented and fill the still-existing information gap about Japan. I read Mr. Sai's book with great pleasure and benefit, and therefore strongly recommend it. I am convinced that great profit can be gained by reading it."

Gottfried Wolf, MS
Senior Executive,
Professorship at the Technical
University, Vienna

"**Y**asutaka Sai has written the ultimate overview of Japanese business, including corporate structure, decision making, and management lifestyles. *The Eight Core Values of the Japanese Businessman* profiles the enigma of Japan, the duality of extremes. This book should be suggested reading for every international businessperson and mandatory reading for anyone working directly with, or relating to, Japan.

The business world needs to acquire at least a working knowledge of the eight values perceived and defined, with extensive references, by Mr. Sai. The writer's approach, based on the psychological, cultural, and emotional underpinnings of the Japanese businessman, is unique and timely, given the political, societal, and business changes engulfing Japan in the mid-1990s."

William K. Nichoson, MBA
President, Asia Dynamics Group,
Tokyo, Japan

International Business Press
An Imprint of The Haworth Press, Inc.

The Eight Core Values of the Japanese Businessman

Toward an Understanding of Japanese Management

INTERNATIONAL BUSINESS PRESS
Erdener Kaynak, PhD
Executive Editor

New, Recent, and Forthcoming Titles:

International Business Handbook edited by V. H. (Manek) Kirpalani

Sociopolitical Aspects of International Marketing edited by Erdener Kaynak

How to Manage for International Competitiveness edited by Abbas J. Ali

International Business Expansion into Less-Developed Countries: The International Finance Corporation and Its Operations by James C. Baker

Product-Country Images: Impact and Role in International Marketing edited by Nicolas Papadopoulos and Louise A. Heslop

The Global Business: Four Key Marketing Strategies edited by Erdener Kaynak

Multinational Strategic Alliances edited by Refik Culpan

Market Evolution in Developing Countries: The Unfolding of the Indian Market by Subhash C. Jain

A Guide to Successful Business Relations with the Chinese: Opening the Great Wall's Gate by Huang Quanyu, Richard Andrulis, and Chen Tong

Industrial Products: A Guide to the International Marketing Economics Model by Hans Jansson

Euromarketing: Effective Strategies for International Trade and Export edited by Salah S. Hassan and Erdener Kaynak

How to Utilize New Information Technology in the Global Marketplace: A Basic Guide edited by Fahri Karakaya and Erdener Kaynak

International Negotiating: A Primer for American Business Professionals by Michael Kublin

The Eight Core Values of the Japanese Businessman: Toward an Understanding of Japanese Management by Yasutaka Sai

The Eight Core Values of the Japanese Businessman

Toward an Understanding of Japanese Management

Yasutaka Sai

TITLE VI-B

International Business Press
An Imprint of The Haworth Press, Inc.
New York • London

Published by

International Business Press, an Imprint of The Haworth Press, Inc., 10 Alice Street, Binghamton, NY 13904-1580

Paperback edition published in 1996.

Library of Congress Cataloging-in-Publication Data

Sai, Yasutaka, 1930-
   The eight core values of the Japanese businessman : toward an understanding of Japanese management / Yasutaka Sai.
      p.   cm.
   Includes bibliographical references and index.
   ISBN 1-56024-871-8 (alk. paper).
   1. Management–Social aspects–Japan. 2. Social values–Japan. I. Title.
HD70.J3S155 1995
658′.00952–dc20
                                    94-30686
                                       CIP

,35'

CONTENTS

ABOUT THE AUTHOR

Yasutaka Sai is a management consultant to large Japanese corporations, including Kobe Steel and Minolta Camera, and has traveled extensively overseas as a market researcher, director of study missions, and speaker at seminars and conferences. He was Vice President and Director of International Operations/International Research Institute of the Japan Management Association in Tokyo, where he currently serves as Senior Advisor. His current assignments include consulting to the United States-Japan joint research with The Alexander Consulting Group on excellent quality companies. Mr. Sai is a member of the Multi-National Business Study Forum and he has served as a management training instructor at a U.S. military base in Japan. He graduated from Waseda University in Japan and received training from the Stanford University in the United States.

Preface

Many people, both Japanese and non-Japanese, have debated and explained the thoughts and actions of the Japanese from different viewpoints and from both Japanese and non-Japanese perspectives. Extremely few, however, have focused on the values of the Japanese–especially Japanese businesspeople–thus making it difficult for anyone to explain sufficiently enough just what may be motivating them to think or act the way they do or what may be behind the traditional or changing business practice in Japan.

To fill this gap and provide some material that will help enhance understanding of the Japanese businesspersons' ways of thinking and acting, a group of researchers in the Japan Management Association, including the author, undertook a special research project in 1989, and one of the results of this study was the edition of a summary report in Japanese, which later became the basis of this book.

Our research started initially from defining our interpretation of the values of the Japanese businessperson we were about to explore. After some discussion, our group concluded that it would be best to define it as the "psychological, cultural, or emotional underpinnings that influence the behavior and thinking of the Japanese businessperson." The assumption was that although people's "beliefs" or "aspirations" should not be excluded, it would be more practical to focus on those factors which drive the Japanese businessperson to think or act in daily life, both personally and as a member of an organization.

Our research team's next step was to collect as many books, articles, and other source materials that seemed relevant to our subject and to composite as many writers' views and individual voices and information quoted in their writings as possible. Approximately 300 source materials were thus collected and analyzed, including both the Japanese and English materials. Although the Japanese materials were generally in want of descriptions of the values as such, and often required our "reading between the lines," this review of available literature revealed to us enough insights and information on the subject to enable us to sort out and categorize them into eight core values and prepare a preliminary report based on these findings.

We then conducted interviews with university professors and management consultants, as well as businesspersons in Japan and abroad. Here, we were fortunate enough to talk with individuals of different nationalities, including Americans, an Australian, a Chinese, and a Korean, in addition to Japanese. The management consultants interviewed most represented Japan Management Association and its affiliated organizations, the outfits this writer has long been associated with. These interviews contributed to our study in two ways: they provided further insights and perspectives to our work; they also suggested ideas on how the whole study might be better presented to our potential readers. In fact, it was on the basis of their suggestions that we launched the next step of our work–an extended study of literature (some 200 additional pieces of literature). This helped us to bring more examples to our discussion of "Related Trends and Perspectives." We believe this additional input has helped make this book an even more interesting and insightful reading.

This book is the result of the support and encouragement of many individuals, but special mention needs to be made of two names in particular: Mr. Yoshio Hatakeyama of Japan Management Association and Dr. Erdener Kaynak of the International Business Press. I owe a great deal to Hatakeyama for his support in our research study and subsequent publication of the preliminary report in the Japanese language. I am grateful to Dr. Kaynak for his interest in and encouragement for the publication of this book in English.

I must gratefully acknowledge the contributions made by those individuals who shared their time to participate in our personal interviews to review and supplement their information and insights into my work: Ryuji Fukuda; Akira Hattori; Ryokichi Hirono; Mari Ikeda; Yoshitomo Izawa; Tatsuki Mikami; Takayoshi Nakajima; Yoshio Tomisaka; Akira Totoki; Moriaki Tsuchiya; Shigeo Yamamoto; and Jin Wei.

Also of great help were Robert March, William K. Nichoson, and Ernest C. Miller, who took time not only to review the original report but to suggest ways for improvement in style and content. Mr. Miller also helped coordinate the work schedule between the International Business Press and the author.

Two American translators, Robert Mintzer and Cary R. David challenged and helped complete the major part of the translation from Japanese into English–a most difficult task.

Janese Beckwith, a graduate student in Cultural Anthropology at the University of Chicago who was living in Japan, was also a great help as a consultant on content, and in reorganizing and automating my manuscripts, rewriting and polishing the English language expression, and preparing the final draft for publication.

Many more individuals, including my wife, Toyoko Sai, assisted me or offered me words of encouragement, for which I would like to express my heartfelt appreciation. Without their help and encouragement this book would not have been possible.

Yasutaka Sai

Introduction

"The Japanese people are hard to understand"—so say many people from other cultures. Little surprise. Few Japanese are capable of explaining why they think and behave the way they do, either. For centuries, the Japanese were virtually uninformed of the outside world, and it was only after 1868, when Japan started having contact with the outside world, that the Japanese began to learn that their way of thinking and acting was one thing and that there were other ways of doing things. Little wonder that little has been written about the culture and values of Japanese people from a first-person, Japanese point of view, which may have something to do with the persistent lack of understanding between Japanese and other peoples.

What makes understanding the Japanese people so difficult may also be attributed to the fact that their values are, in reality, quite diverse and often polarized—perhaps much like most other peoples of the world. For example, while on the one hand extolling diligence as a virtue, some Japanese are simultaneously loath to work—especially in situations where they cannot expect appropriate compensation for their labors. Or, while giving precedence to actions that benefit the group over the individual, the Japanese tend to act, too, with a concern for the benefit of the individual. Especially in recent years, a dramatic shift is taking place in the thinking of the average worker away from the earlier orientation of an almost exclusive devotion to the job or company toward a growing concern for the individual and the family.

The same person who is meticulous about keeping his own yard clean may feel no compunction against throwing his or her trash into a vacant lot next door. Or the same individual who teaches his or her children to live "true to yourself" may be found hypocritically spouting "tatemae" (the official line) niceties aimed primarily at pleasing others. Such double standards are part of life in Japan.

In her book, *The Chrysanthemum and the Sword*, anthropologist Ruth Benedict wrote:

> During the past seventy-five years since Japan's closed doors were opened, the Japanese have been described in the most fantastic series of "but also's" ever used for any nation of the world. When a serious observer is writing about peoples other than the Japanese and says they are unprecedentedly polite, he is not likely to add, "But also insolent and overbearing." When he says people of some nation are incomparably rigid in their behavior, he does not add, "But also they adapt themselves readily to extreme innovations." When he says a people are submissive, he does not explain too that they are not easily amenable to control from above. When he says they are loyal and generous, he does not declare, "But also treacherous and spiteful." When he says they are genuinely brave, he does not expatiate on their timidity. When he says they act out of concern for others' opinions, he does not then go on to tell that they have a truly terrifying conscience. When he describes robot-like discipline in their Army, he does not continue by describing the way the soldiers in that Army take the bit in their own teeth even to the point of insubordination. . . .
>
> All these contradictions, however, are the warp and woof of books on Japan. They are true. Both the sword and the chrysanthemum are a part of the picture. The Japanese are, to the highest degree, both aggressive and unaggressive, both militaristic and aesthetic, both insolent and polite, rigid and adaptable, submissive and resentful of being pushed around, loyal and treacherous, brave and timid, conservative and hospitable to new ways. They are terribly concerned about what other people will think of their behavior, and they are also overcome by guilt when other people know nothing of their misstep. Their soldiers are disciplined to the hilt but are also insubordinate.[1]

This dual "both extremes" nature of Japanese thought, values, and behavior, while being human nature in part, may be confusing in the end to non-Japanese, and add to the impression of exoticism and evasiveness that they already have of Japanese.

Yet, mysterious as they may seem, all people are alike. With a proper knowledge of the social and cultural underpinnings of business practices in Japan, it would not be very difficult for non-Japanese to understand and move confidently among Japanese. Indeed, many have successfully bridged this cultural gap already.

In this book several attempts have been made to help understand the seemingly complicated values of the Japanese businesspeople. First, discussion focuses on eight specific values that are most commonly shared by Japanese in the business world: group orientation; diligence; aesthetics and perfectionism; curiosity and emphasis on innovation; respect for form; a mind for competition and outlook on reward; the importance of silence; and perceptions of time. Because of the broadness of these values and their implications, and again for ease of understanding, the topic of group orientation was explored by bringing to light several other related dimensions, i.e., sense of belonging and participation, and spirit of harmony and interpersonal relations. Likewise, the chapter on diligence includes sections on the Japanese work ethic and "stick-to-it" attitude on the job. Readers are reminded that, while the eight values discussed in this book are clearly among the most prevalent or most widely shared, they are not meant to be the only values, or the most important ones Japanese businesspeople have. Just as other businesspeoples of the world do, Japanese businesspeople have more values to share than these eight. As can be expected, individuals vary in the amount of importance they attach to certain values over others.

Second, in discussing these values, frequent reference is made to the values of the "average" Japanese citizen in regard to the ingrained customs and mores of Japanese business organizations. Basically, Japanese people inside and outside of business share the same values, even if the former may, being in a business environment, embrace some values more strongly. Therefore, beliefs and values of people in business may have slightly different nuances from those of the average person.

Finally, in discussing Japanese corporate culture, an attempt has been made to present as many specific examples as possible. After all, the values of an individual are best illustrated by what he or she says or does, and the Japanese, although group oriented, are no exception.

A number of theories have been advanced concerning the sources of the Japanese values and ways of thinking discussed in this book. Some propose that the origins of Japanese culture can be traced back to the rice-paddy culture of the Yayoi Period circa 300 B.C. Others see its roots in the particular kind of "family system" born from time, isolation from other cultures, and the particular life experience of the Japanese, be it geographic, climatic, political, biological, and all the forces that make a particular people what they are.

A long history of poverty and the numerous natural disasters—earthquakes, tsunami, floods, droughts, and so on—that have regularly afflicted the archipelago through its history have also been cited as principle influences on Japanese values.

Another popular theory suggests that Japanese values ultimately derived from religious influences, whether those of Japan's native Shintoism or those of Buddhism and Confucianism, both of which entered Japan during the sixth century.

Finally, more than a few see Japanese culture, particularly in the context of the business world, as an outgrowth of various historical events such as the Meiji Restoration of 1868, the Imperial Edict on Education in 1890 which greatly expanded access to education, or the influx of Western thought after 1945 and the social changes that followed.

There is no single uniformly accepted source for the values of today's Japanese citizen or businessperson. As with all cultures, modern Japanese thinking must be a product of a combination of all these factors. However, the vast majority of Japanese still support the view that, at least until very recently, economic deprivation has been the most influential factor in the thinking and behavior of the Japanese people.

REFERENCE NOTE

1. Ruth Benedict, 1974. *The Chrysanthemum and the Sword*. Tokyo: Charles E. Tuttle Co.

Chapter 1

Group Orientation

Three ordinary people put together can think of a better plan than one Manjushiri.
(Manjushiri is said to have been a Buddhist priest renowned for his profound wisdom)

The stake that sticks out will be hammered down.

IMPORTANCE OF GROUP RELATIONSHIPS

In contrast to Western individualism, the Japanese are typically fond of doing things together in groups, whether eating, drinking, playing, studying, or working. If there is a choice, they choose to live where others are living. Many Japanese feel that being a member of an organized group–be it a club of schoolmates or a neighborhood committee–is the most pleasurable and comfortable human experience. This feeling of mutual pleasure and comfort grows stronger as people are associated with the same group members for a long time. The older the group alliances are, the greater the mutual enjoyment when group members are together.

Japanese are socialized from early childhood to consider themselves members of a group–as interdependent members of family, school, community, and other collectives. Parents teach children to play together with others, and kindergarten teachers discipline them to suppress individual desires in favor of the rules of the particular group. In Japan, to be well adjusted one must fit into many social groups harmoniously rather than stand out.

Japanese are also taught that group action can yield a far more productive result than individual action. For example, Motonari Mori, a feudal shogun and philosopher, is known to have quoted this ancient maxim to his three sons: "When bound together, shafts of bamboo become strong enough to make a solid arrow; yet when divided they are nothing more than a bundle of sticks which hardly serve any practical purpose at all." The same idea is expressed in the American saying: "United we stand, divided we fall."

Thus, many Japanese place a high value on group conformity and, through this, group order, stability, and overall progress. The well-being of one's group comes before the well-being of the individual.

There are some self-centered Japanese, of course. One tends to find such individuals among artists, craftspeople, or specialists of one kind or another–those who prefer living by their own standards rather than blindly following others. Individual expression is sometimes socially acceptable. Some Japanese women, for example, have a highly individual style of dressing or speaking. And, as in most parts of the world, young people in Japan often resist traditional group norms.

The origin of Japanese emphasis on groups rather than individuals has been attributed to many factors. One explanation points to Japan's traditional rice culture in which centuries of constant interdependence and cooperation were needed among farming communities (see Photo 1.1). Another theory has it that the frequent occurrence of natural disasters in Japanese history, such as earthquakes, floods, and droughts, demanded collective interdependence among the country's populace. The consensus among Japanese is that the fear of attack from neighboring countries also must have contributed to the strong bonding of the Japanese, as did a sense of linguistic isolation along with a fear of being unable to communicate adequately with foreigners. One theory has it that although Japanese are basically optimistic, once they feel a threat, they can instantly turn pessimistic and unite against an enemy.

In contrast, Arthur M. Whitehill, Professor of International Management at the University of Hawaii, offers the following regarding American individualism: "(It) is traced to a frontier psychology. The early pioneers, pushing west through an uncharted and hostile environment, had only themselves to rely upon. It was 'every man for himself,' and individuals survived by their own wits and ambition. . . . "[1]

PHOTO 1.1. When a farmer starts planting young rice-plants, it is common for his neighbors to come to help the farmer get the job done—on a reciprocal basis. *(Courtesy of Japan Management Association)*

On the corporate level, businesspeople share this group orientation in a number of ways. Most individuals enjoy the comfort and security of being together with others in a work group. The rules of the group and of the work to be completed take precedence over individual interests. Most people have a personal desire to work hard to attain group objectives through mutual efforts. Here, again, group values are given priority over individual values.

The following is a set of basic Japanese group values and the individual behaviors and company practices that reflect them in everyday business environments.

Group Identity

When introducing themselves, Japanese businesspersons describe themselves first as members of a group, and then give their names within the context of their position in the company. For example, "I am from Hitachi. My name is Sato. I am with the Human Resources Department." Similarly, they often identify individuals with the organizations they represent–such as "Honda's Mr. Yamada."

Open Office Plan

Most offices in Japan reflect an open plan, with all the desks of the department or section being arranged close together in clusters in a large room with few or no partitions. Japanese staff feel comfortable working in crowded, noisy conditions (see Photo 1.2). "Why not?" they might ask. "It is good for communication and teamwork. Besides, if someone accidentally had a heart attack at his or her desk, it would be in everyone's sight immediately."

Honda is famous for having company officers share the one large open office. And companies adopting this single-executive office style are on the increase.

Once-a-Year Hiring

Japanese organizations, especially large corporations, make it a practice to hire new recruits all at once, in April of each year, rather than interviewing and taking job applicants throughout the year.

These companies are also reluctant to accept mid-career job applicants for various reasons; after all, they may not have "fit in" with previous employers. The loyalty of a mid-level hire is questionable, and it is easier to develop workers within the group from scratch. Also, there is a fear that these new workers may be discriminated against by existing staff, including managers. Possible discrimination may go something like this: "Why are these 'outsiders' getting better pay than us? These guys may be more senior than us, but we have been employed here longer than they!"

In addition, many companies provide collective training–an induction into organizational structure, philosophy, strategies, etc.– for a period from several weeks to several months. Not only is this practice of once-a-year hiring and group induction cost effective for the employer, but it is considered to be conducive to developing a sense of group loyalty among new entrants. This initiation practice

PHOTO 1.2. Most Japanese office staff feel comfortable working in crowded conditions, usually in a large room. *(Courtesy of Japan Management Association)*

encourages a sense of comradeship and, at times, of healthy competition.

Long-Term Commitment

Across the board, Japanese employers expect their newly hired to stay with them throughout their lifetime as loyal workers. The new entrants, on their part, also aspire to work for the same organization for the rest of their lives. Therefore, both sides indicate a willingness to be "married" to the company on a long-term basis, although such commitment is seldom written into any formal contract. This mutual expectation of long-term employment typically applies mainly to male workers in large organizations, although more and more women are being included in this practice.

The so-called "lifetime commitment" is a practice that was initiated by employers, rather than by employees, as a means to attract and secure necessary labor during times of a tight labor market. This practice, in fact, has its roots in the early days of industrial expansion following the Meiji Restoration and opening to the West in 1868, and again during the post World War II period. Medium to small businesses generally find it difficult to offer lifetime employment and expensive benefits, and consequently tend to have higher staff turnover and employ more part-timers.

Assignment to Work Group–Not Job

After a period of orientation, individual entrants are assigned to different workplaces, usually as members of some office, department, or section; rarely are they assigned to a specific job or position. Often awaiting the newly hired is a *jirei*, a brief note officially admitting him or her to a specific office, department, or section of the organization, and some gesture of welcome by senior colleagues of the new workplace. There is no specific job description for individual entrants; nor are their responsibilities clearly defined.

Group Mission Statement

Some companies, usually the large ones, do have some statement of mission or of roles that management expects of each department or section. Where such statements are available, newly hired employees are supposed to go through them to find out on their own just what is expected of the employee in the next few years at least, as a member of the particular group he or she has been assigned to.

Teamwork

For most Japanese workers nothing is so important as teamwork in the workplace. They take it for granted to do work with a team effort and, in fact, exert every effort for the sake of a team project under someone's leadership. There are occasionally disagreements or conflicts of opinion among group members, but usually "a stake that sticks out gets hammered down."

On the other hand, team unity tends to be strengthened when members see some sign of competition between them and other teams. As a matter of fact, some team leaders purposely induce competition among their members so that the work group may be motivated to demonstrate a greater team spirit.

One important difference between this Japanese tendency and some American business tendencies is that, as a rule, Japanese do not personalize relationships with those on the other side of a bargaining table. In this respect, an observation made by Robert March, an international negotiation consultant, deserves attention:

> In my observations of many Japanese negotiation teams, from pre-negotiation to caucus-period discussions, they have ranged from highly experienced to inexperienced. In spite of this wide difference, I detect certain characteristics that reflect how the culture itself predisposes even naive and inexperienced Japanese businessmen to negotiate in a secure, parsimonious, and cautious manner.

[for example:]

> As a rule, the Japanese always form cohesive teams, even if composed of strangers. These teams may not always be well led or well managed, but they do have clear leaders whose leadership is respected, in contrast to Western teams where everyone wants to be a negotiator and leadership often becomes nominal and cohesion minimal. Japanese team membership is also more flexible in that fresh players can be readily substituted.

> *Position:* Developing a unified team position and then getting consensus, i.e., the support of the whole team for the position adopted, generates even greater team cohesion and support for the leader.

> *Bargaining:* Once a firm position is achieved, the Japanese strongly commit themselves to it and give little thought to bargaining, or making concessions to achieve their goals. Most Japanese negotiators I have spoken to, however, do say that they are usually prepared to give modest concessions, perhaps 10 percent or so, but they tend to feel offended if a Westerner asks for 30-40 percent concessions, because this

means the foreigner is assuming that the Japanese have made an initial offer far different from what they are really prepared to accept.

Lack of Hurry: The lack of a sense of deadlines or pressure of time makes the Japanese supremely calm.

In looking at how American and other Western businessmen manage negotiations, there is no doubt that they are often vulnerable on each of these points and are easily intimidated by apparent Japanese solidarity. In contrast to the Japanese, their teamwork is poor and their position fragile, not considered or secured. Thus they easily make concessions in the mere hope of reciprocity, thus damaging their own position. Finally, they can be in such a hurry that they make concessions merely to meet some arbitrary deadline.[2]

In Japanese companies it is not unusual to see this teamwork being staged across departmental boundaries. One video-cassette recorder (VCR) manufacturer, faced with the need to increase its VCR production expeditiously, had the company's research and development, design, and manufacturing departments join forces to study the feasibility of parts procurement, high-precision fabrication, and set assembly as a group. As a result, the company turned out millions of VCRs in a matter of several months.

Group-Oriented Evaluation and Compensation

Japanese systems of employee evaluation and compensation, particularly the latter, reflect management emphasis on group performance rather than individual performance. Employees are evaluated, and their salaries determined, more on the basis of how well they have performed as a member of the group, or how much an individual has contributed to group performance, than on their own merits.

Determining relative contribution to one's group, however, usually involves more individual- than job- or position-related factors, such as education, age, length of service, and gender. This is in addition to group performance factors such as loyalty to one's organization, good faith, effort, cooperativeness, and willingness to take responsibilities for the sake of one's group, depending on areas of work responsibilities (research laboratories, factory assembly lines, sales, etc.) and position (see Tables 1.1 and 1.2).

Promotion, too, tends to be based on one's contribution to the group. The one who wins recognition for outstanding effort and respect by others has a better chance to get promoted ahead of his peers.

Employees' monthly salaries are linked primarily to length of service, which provides a sense of fairness in a seniority-oriented society. Individual accomplishments tend to be reflected more directly in the mid-year and year-end bonuses, although utmost care is exercised to assure that this extra income will become motivational not only for the individuals concerned but for the group as a whole.

Finally, the monthly pay package also includes a wide variety of allowances designed to meet individual needs, such as family size, housing, and transportation expenses.

Fringe Benefits

Japanese companies offer their employees and their families a variety of fringe benefits such as company housing or help with a mortgage, seaside or mountain resort facilities, low interest real estate loans, support of baseball or other sports teams, sponsorship of flower arrangement classes, foreign language study programs, funding for company staff cafeteria or concession dining rooms, in-house medical services, lump-sum retirement packages, and so on. The idea here is to provide additional incentives for employees and their families to enjoy being a part of the total company family group.

Few Layoffs

In the minds of many Japanese, an organization is a community. Not only is it a great shame for any employer to lay off or fire employees, but it is considered to be a disgrace to the community in which it operates. It is, in a way, a breach of the "gentleman's agreement" between the employer and the employee concerning employment. Besides, in a society of near-zero mobility, workers who have been laid off are likely to have great economic difficulty.

TABLE 1.1. Size of Firm and Average Annual Wage in the Private Sector in Japan (1989)[a]

	Male		Female		Average No. of Years Employed	
	Monthly Wage Total	Annual Total[b]	Monthly Wage Total	Annual Total[b]	Male	Female
	(¥1,000)	(¥1,000)	(¥1,000)	(¥1,000)		
Individual Enterprises	2,908	3,285	1,626	1,925	11.6	11.6
Capitalization: Under ¥10 million	3,869	4,431	1,955	2,232	11.0	8.9
¥10 million–	3,773	4,614	1,851	2,241	11.0	7.2
¥50 million–	3,777	4,856	1,794	2,249	11.5	6.3
¥100 million–	3,882	5,236	1,838	2,398	13.1	6.3
¥1,000 million–	4,464	6,286	2,112	2,921	16.6	7.6
Total[c]	4,013	5,188	1,925	2,401	13.0	7.5
Other Legal Entities	3,613	4,375	2,043	2,526	11.6	9.1
Total	**3,876**	**4,928**	**1,908**	**2,358**	**12.7**	**8.7**

a) Labor force coverage: full-time employees at private establishments. In 1989 the labor force so defined was 38.47 million people. b) Monthly Wage Total and Total Bonus. c) *Kabushiki-kaisha* or limited liability establishments.
Source: National Tax Administration Agency, Japan.

Consequently, most companies resort to various actions to avoid employee layoff or dismissal. For example, curtailment of hiring, encouragement of early retirement, lending of company staff to other organizations including subsidiaries and subcontractors, sending home redundant employees, placing them "on call" until conditions improve, and so forth. Some companies even go so far as to enforce a 10 to 20 percent cut in all management salaries right up to the top. Any employer who fails to take such remedial steps and who resorts to the dismissal of employees frequently is, in Japan, likely to invite social censure. Worse, such an employer can lose trust from the labor force in its industry, and suffer severe difficulty

TABLE 1.2. Hourly Wages in Manufacturing Industry (1970, 1990)

	Hourly Wages (National Currency/Hour)			US$/Hour[a]
	Unit	1970	1990	1990
U.S.A.	(US$)	3.35	10.83	10.83
Canada	(C$)	3.01	14.30	12.26
Japan	**(Yen)**	**336**	**1,993[e]**	**13.76[b]**
Sweden	(S. Korone)	12.17	73.20	12.37
Germany, F.R.	(D. Mark)	5.96	20.07	12.42
Belgium	(B. Franc)	–	327.13[c]	8.30
Italy	(Lira)	635	9,451[d]	4.95
U.K.	(Pound)	0.55	5.384	9.61
New Zealand	(NZ$)	–	13.43	8.02
France	(F. Franc)	5.92	43.43[c]	6.81

a) U.S. dollar figures are calculated according to the annual average exchange rates of the IMF, *International Financial Statistics*. b) US$1.00=¥144.79 (1990). c) 1989. d) 1985. e) Hourly wages = Monthly average gross wages ÷ Monthly average hours worked. Companies employing 30 or more.
Source: ILO, *Bulletin of Labour Statistics*, 1991-4; Ministry of Labour, Japan. Monthly Labor Survey

in attracting quality workers when the time comes for it to recruit workers again.

During the oil crisis of the 1970s, Sony plants in the United States were faced with the need to curtail operations at one of its newly built factories in California. The company's American executives felt that layoffs were inevitable, but after consulting with their partners in Japan they decided not to let anyone go until the very last moment of possible bankruptcy. The result was that the company had to close one factory for some days, but had their workers report to the factory to clean their workplaces or participate in specially conducted training programs, and the company was able to pay their salaries during the entire period of the plant shutdown[3] (see Table 1.3).

Company Unions

Most of the Japanese labor unions are "company unions" rather than "trade unions." Independent as they are from management at least nominally, they are physically and psychologically a part of the company. The members of the union are the members of the company, sharing both union interests and company interests at the same time.

Under these circumstances, union members by and large are quite cooperative with management. If a company decides to adopt robotics for some of its operations, for example, union members will be among the first to consider implementing it in all seriousness. "We are all in this together," they might say. The idea of opposing such a proposition on the grounds of a possible threat to job security would never occur to them. Both unions and their members are more interested in gaining a greater share of the pie than in participating in a non-productive union activity such as a walkout or a strike (see Table 1.4).

Extensive Information Sharing

Japanese businesspeople place great store on collecting and sharing information of common interest such as news about their competitors. This information sharing becomes particularly important when one needs support or understanding from others concerned with a certain proposition. The logic behind this is that the better people are informed, the more likely they will cooperate. This is what "nemawashi" (spade work or lobbying) is all about.

The giving and taking of news and information frequently takes place in formal meetings as well. In fact, most of the meetings held by Japanese are, for some people, primarily to present what others would be interested in knowing before discussing or making decisions as suggested by agenda. Meetings are often prolonged due to this emphasis on information sharing.

TABLE 1.3. Unemployment: Number and Rate (1985-1991)

		Japan	U.S.A.[a]	Germany, F.R.	France[a]	U.K.
Number (1,000)	1985	**1,560**	8,312	2,304	2,394	3,271
	1986	**1,670**	8,237	2,228	2,517	3,289
	1987	**1,730**	7,425	2,229	2,836	2,953
	1988	**1,550**	6,700	2,242	2,564	2,370
	1989	**1,420**	6,520	2,038	2,532	1,799
	1990	**1,340**	6,873	1,883	2,503	1,665
	1991 May	**1,360**	8,640	1,604	2,689	2,214
Rate (%)	1985	**2.6**	7.2	9.3	10.2	11.8
	1986	**2.8**	7.0	9.0	10.4	11.8
	1987	**2.8**	6.2	8.9	10.5	10.6
	1988	**2.5**	5.5	8.7	10.0	8.5
	1989	**2.3**	5.3	7.9	9.4	6.3
	1990	**2.1**	5.5	7.2	8.9	5.9
	1991 May	**2.1**	6.9	6.0	9.3	7.8

a) Seasonally adjusted.
Source: Bank of Japan, *Comparative International Statistics*, 1991; Economic Statistics Monthly.

Follow-the-Leader Syndrome

Perhaps as a consequence of their group orientation, Japanese people and their companies have a strong propensity to follow in the footsteps of a leader or some other role model instead of taking the initiative on their own. To act differently from others, or "going my own way," tends to invite group pressure to conform–as the

TABLE 1.4. Days Lost in Labor Disputes (1980-1990)[a]

	U.S.A.	Italy	U.K.	France	Japan[b]	Germany, F.R.
1980	20,844	16,457	11,964	1,511	998	128
1981	16,908	10,527	4,266	1,442	543	58
1982	9,061	18,563	5,313	2,257	535	15
1983	17,461	14,003	3,754	1,321	504	41
1984	8,499	8,703	27,135	1,318	354	5,618
1985	7,079	3,831	6,402	727	257	35
1986	12,140	5,644	1,920	568	252	28
1987	4,469	4,606	3,546	501	256	33
1988	4,364	3,315	3,702	1,132	163	42
1989	16,996	4,436	4,128	805	176	100
1990	5,926	–	1,880	–	–	–

a) Based on data from each country. Labor disputes, as a rule, involve protest action. b) Japanese figures include days of disputes involving protest action and factory closure.
Source: Bank of Japan, *Comparative International Statistics*, 1991.

saying goes, "the stake that sticks out gets hammered down." And, because of this discrimination by the majority against the minority, many end up choosing a seemingly more peaceful and profitable course of action, resulting in "follow-the-leader" or "keep up with the Joneses" tendencies.

Masamoto Yashiro of Citibank Japan has this to say: "If [a firm's conduct is] seen to be unfavorable from an industry standpoint, pressures are exercised, not only by private companies but also from the government. . . ."[4]

For example, Sony Corporation is one of the few companies in Japan influential enough to make industry innovations. But even Sony runs the risk of suffering from pressure to conform to industry protocol. Sony chairman Akio Morita recently commented, "If one single company tried to renovate something, it would never undertake aggressive efforts. Instead, they would choose to prioritize their own protection."[5] One could interpret Morita's comments as reflecting recently publicized Sony policies to break with tradition by (1) not asking potential new employees what university they graduated from, and (2) by producing more durable products rather than following the industry practice of frequently introducing new products.

Examples of this conservative tendency are plentiful. In the brewery industry, after Asahi introduced a new type of beer called "super dry" with good success, other brewery companies followed suit, and all with similar brand labels, emphasizing the newness of their products. Another example can be found in the automotive industry. During the past several years, one major Japanese automobile manufacturer after another started pouring so many different models and brands of cars into the market that the number of passenger car names has nearly doubled (see table below). One consequence of this is that the industry is being criticized for its apparent obsession to "keep up with the Joneses," rather than respond to real consumer demand.

Comparison of Passenger Car Brands by Automaker[6]

	Toyota	Nissan	Mitsubishi	Matsuda
January, 1987	20	21	8	9
August, 1992	25	23	12	24

Industrial Group System

As ardent followers of the "united we stand" principle of Motonari Mori, Japanese companies are enthusiastic about looking for ways of alliance. The powerful *zaibatsus* (financial cliques) of the prewar era created by long-established merchant families like Mitsubishi, Mitsui, and Sumitomo, are world famous. After the war, a looser form of company affiliation began to appear, giving rise to present-day industrial group systems.

Today's Japanese corporate organizations come in two basic varieties–"industrial groups" and "keiretsu groups." The industrial groups are based on horizontal ties between companies in different industries, and among them are the three descendants of the prewar zaibatsu plus Fuyo, Sanwa, and Daiichi Kangyo Bank. Keiretsu groups are characterized by vertical links with a large manufacturer at the core. Included in the 17 or so keiretsu groups of today are names like Fujitsu, Hitachi, Matsushita Electric, NEC, Nippon Steel, Nissan, Toshiba, and Toyota.

Mutual advantage is the name of the alliance game. The group ties contribute to stability as well as allowing members to achieve maximum efficiency in producing goods requiring a wide range of parts and components–as in automobiles.

Passive View Toward Company Consolidation

Notwithstanding the above-mentioned propensity to form groups of common interest, Japanese managers are not as aggressive as their Western counterparts in pursuing industrial consolidation such as mergers and acquisitions. Traditional Japanese paternalism, or familism, often makes it difficult to reach a consensus on the pursuit of a proposed "cross-breeding" with other "species." Mitsui Toatsu and Mitsui Petrochemical, the two companies that have been affiliated with the same Mitsui Group, share a number of the same shareholders and even share the building for their offices. They have been deadlocked in their talks on a possible merger for months at the time of this writing. As one reporter comments, "each company has too distinct a corporate culture."

Intra-Group Competition

The Japanese are generally loath to lag behind others or to be thought of as inferior to others, and this feeling tends to be strong among members of the same group where comradeship is strong. Business organizations are no exception, with different units within the same company or different enterprises within the same line of business trying to outdo each other in order to secure a strong position or standing within the group. A fierce competition among rival companies in terms of price, brand name, delivery date, after sale service, etc., is a phenomenon common to Japanese industries both in Japan and abroad.

A SENSE OF BELONGING

As already noted, the Japanese aspire to belong to some group or groups of people rather than to be alone. Unlike Americans who move around routinely, most Japanese are hesitant to leave the place where they have settled down. Young adults feel comfortable living with their parents even after they have reached the age of 20. Families dislike changing their homes or relocating to new, unknown areas, and workers feel comfortable working for the same employers and in the same workplaces for a lifetime. Even after travel abroad on business, most Japanese quickly return home to Japan.

The initial goal of Japanese businesspersons is to find some identifiable place of work–a company or similar organization–and to nestle in and stay there as long as possible. They expect that wherever their work may be, they can find both a personal challenge and a sense of community there. The sense of "shared fate" is strong once a commitment to a group is made, sharing feelings of pleasure or sadness with colleagues throughout life. In this sense, the company becomes a kind of emotional "home" for employees, and team members become like family. It is for these reasons that some employees get married and hold other family-oriented, life-changing events in their company building.

Spring begins with cherry blossoms in Japan. People set up a picnic area in a popular place to view cherry blossoms, drink and eat, and even sing under the trees, often on weekday evenings. Among these cherry viewers during weekdays here and there are youngsters in their business suits who are waiting for their company mates to join them after work. These youngsters are usually newly hired company employees who have been sent out in the early morning with orders to locate and save the best possible viewing spots for the sake of their senior members (see Photo 1.3). When successful, the young scouts are given much credit, a sign of being accepted by the group.

Members of Japanese companies generally believe in the impor-

PHOTO 1.3. During the spring cherry-viewing season, young company staff are seen saving viewing spots for the sake of their senior members who will later join them after work in the evening. *(Courtesy of Japan Management Association)*

tance of instilling a sense of belonging in their employees. Says one senior manager of a large manufacturing company: "The Japanese have such strong potential for a sense of belonging that it would be a shame if we did not develop it. Our managers' job is to make sure workers feel happy not only about doing a job but doing it with a sense of belonging."

Japanese companies have developed a variety of systems for encouraging, directly or indirectly, a sense of belonging in their employees. Incentives include lifetime employment, low interest loans, and yearly bonuses. Some companies even provide a company graveyard for their employees.

This focus on the employees' sense of belonging is fruitful in many ways. For example, workers tend to feel as if it is their duty to be loyal to the company. Managers tend to be willing to accept a company order to relocate and work away from their families for a few years, as a "business bachelor." When invited, few employees resist joining in the so-called "small-group" of the workplace, and participating in its activities, more or less voluntarily.

Akio Morita, chairman of Sony, has this story to tell to indicate how the benefit of the company is often integrated into the individual's thoughts even after hours.

> One morning on her way to work, an employee at NEC's Kumamoto Factory was waiting at a railway crossing just in front of the plant as a long freight train passed. As the train rolled by her, she began to notice how strong pulsating vibrations seemed to pass right through her feet. She began to wonder whether the same vibrations might not be having adverse effects on the products being made in the factory.
>
> She recalled how her factory, for some unknown reason, always had a higher defect rate than other NEC factories. And no matter how hard she and her co-workers kept trying, they were consistently unable to lower the defect rate beyond a certain level. Every day all employees, from the plant manager down, had been meeting to discuss the problem. Although she knew that she was personally unaware of any vibrations present in the factory, she began to wonder whether such vibrations might nevertheless be affecting the factory's sensitive manufacturing equipment.
>
> That morning after she arrived at work she mentioned the incident to her foreman, who in turn reported it to the plant manager. The plant manager took swift action and had a long, deep trench dug between the railway tracks and the factory, which he had filled with water. After that the defect rate plummeted—and all because of a few words from an 18-year-old employee.[7]

A SENSE OF PARTICIPATION

For most Japanese, not only is a sense of belonging important but a sense of participation as well. Because group efforts often reap more than what the individual can expect on his or her own, many Japanese prefer to participate in group activities. Eizaburo Nishibori, leader of Japan's first hibernal expedition to the South Pole in 1956, noted:

> When I spent the winter in the Antarctic with a team of ten members, we went into the work with the mutual determination to make our project a success. And it was this singleness of purpose that brought the disparate personalities of the group together in a mutual cooperative effort. We were able to succeed in our first wintering project by giving every person in the group encouragement to make them feel that everybody else appreciated their efforts.[8]

In the business environment, Japanese tend to be particularly conscious of participation and most place a strong sense of personal value on "getting involved" or "getting things done with others" in some teams or projects. Many would gladly participate if it is deemed to be in the best interest of an organization to which they belong, and would respond with an extra outpouring of energy if there is some rivalry around–like a "tug-of-war" situation. Few businesspersons will refuse an opportunity to have a shared feeling of unity that may be derived from participation. Japanese management, on its part, feels responsible for providing employees with as many and varied opportunities for employee participation as possible, as shown in the following examples.

Emphasis on Bottom-Up Communication

A common ideal in any Japanese organization is that, to be successful, there should be a good understanding of the ideas and values shared among all of its members, regardless of status and position in the organizational hierarchy. In most Japanese organizations, however, employees in the lower echelons tend to keep their opinions to themselves, especially in public, due, perhaps, to intimidation or respect for their superiors. Under these circumstances, many Japanese managers try to ensure that their subordinates' voices are sufficiently expressed by providing a time and place for younger employees to learn to become more assertive and articulate in public or among company members. After all, managers fear that where there is not enough communication, there can be no real feeling of participation, and that can be to the detriment of everyone in the group.

Some Japanese companies make a special effort to draw out employees' ideas or feelings one way or the other. One large manufacturing company in Osaka, for example, has a policy under which each officer of the company is supposed to get together with ten of their employees regularly, solely for the purpose of information sharing. There are other organizations, too, which follow a practice of getting their workers to write and submit to management, more or less regularly, a paper which they variously call, "My Vision of the Future," or "Our Company's Issues as I See Them," etc. (see p. 28, Opinion Survey). Again, the belief is that the more you have a chance to say something about company matters, the stronger your sense of participation becomes.

Group Decision Making

For similar reasons, Japanese companies continue the tradition of involving a number of responsible staff–usually mid to senior management staff–in making various decisions. Many decision-making meetings take an inordinate length of time as a result. The following is a remark by Naomi Yamaki, President of Mitsubishi Space Software:

> Even in cases where management is capable of formulating viable solutions to problems on its own, this is not done because to hand down decisions from top to bottom would run counter to a company's group orientation and negate the advantages to be reaped from employees' regular participation. . . . Participation in the decision process by numerous participants facilitates the smooth and swift execution of any decisions reached, and thus is effective in achieving the cooperation of employees which leads to the desired results.[9]

Autonomous Activities

In a growing number of Japanese companies, managers are called on not only to participate in the company-sponsored "management development program," but as part of such training, to start analyzing problems and finding solutions for certain company issues at hand, by themselves. Often, the process involves the company president initially formulating the "management policies of the year," and then department managers developing "department policies of the year," and finally project leaders writing up "project plans of the year," and so on, ending up with individual projects being implemented and their results made known to everyone concerned toward the end of each fiscal year. Minolta Camera reports that as a result of such "voluntary activities," productivity in one of its factories during a certain year jumped ten times higher than in a normal year.

Autonomous management, in the usual sense of the term, is also common. For example, in Matsushita Electric Industrial Company, the world's largest manufacturer of consumer electric goods, the so-called division system was first instituted in 1932, based on its late founder Konosuke Matsushita's philosophy that "every person in the company is responsible for management." Today, Matsushita is just one of many companies in Japan where every one of its hundreds of offices and plants throughout Japan is an autonomous managerial unit within each division, with a system of accounting much like that of an independent company.[10]

Small Group Activity

Both "small group" and "small group activity" have long been buzzwords in Japanese industry. "Small group" here denotes a group of ten to 15 workers in the same workshop–usually the factory. The group members share the same tasks to perform or the same issues to tackle and often get together informally–sometimes after work–to exchange information and ideas, or just to study together (see Photo 1.4). It is not unusual for a factory to have a total of 20 to 30 such small groups active at one time. In fact, at the time of this writing, Honda is known to have more than 10,000 such groups, consisting of over 100,000 workers worldwide.

Interestingly, one such "small group," or "QC Circle" as it is popularly known, evolved in Japan as a by-product of the introduction in Japan of an American control technique called "statistical

PHOTO 1.4. A group of 10 to 15 workers in the same workshop meet regularly—and often informally—to discuss ideas, solve problems, or just to study together. *(Courtesy of Japan Management Association)*

quality control" after World War II. Explains Takayoshi Nakajima of JMA Consultants in Tokyo:

> When exposed to statistical quality control (SQC), Japanese workers were initially quite negative toward it, by and large because of its reliance on statistics. However, once they discovered that SQC offered them new opportunities for participation, their attitude grew quite positive and their participation self-motivated. Eventually the emphasis on statistics was shelved, and this marked the beginning of Japan's famed "Quality Control Circle."

The statistical quality control technique was first introduced in Japan in 1949 by Dr. W. E. Deming. As implied by T. Nakajima, it has been conducive to the creation of the so-called "QC Circles" in millions of Deming adherent factories in Japan since 1962.

The significance of this "small group activity" lies in the fact that it affords workers an opportunity to participate in group activities fairly easily, motivating almost every worker on the shop floor.

This was again substantiated when the "Zero Defect Program," another American-born management approach, was imported into Japan around 1965. Japanese factories took advantage of this new program–and many still do–primarily as a means to reduce product parts defects, but more importantly, as another challenge to which the company's "small group activity" might be geared. The result, in many cases, has been a success. The ZD Program proves to be an effective way to motivate employees to achieve specific goals, and to stimulate competition among them to come up with new ideas.

Opinion Survey

Sadaharu Sato, upon taking office as President of Sumitomo Kaiun (marine transport), found that the company workers had not in the least been involved in company matters. The first thing that had to be done was to bring these people back on track–"to invite them to appear on the same 'dohyo' (sumo wrestling ground)."

By Sato's order, a questionnaire was designed and sent out to all the company staff, and to Sato's surprise half of 380 employees responded–some with nothing but criticisms or complaints about the company, but most with some comments on their own weaknesses. Sato lost no time in informing them about the results of the survey, and initiating actions that would meet employee expectations.

The result: "It was hard to believe . . . the company's monthly deficit of half a million yen that had persisted for years in the past, now became nil within a matter of six months. . . ."[11]

The Spirit of Harmony

As proclaimed in the first article of Japan's one-time constitution, "harmony is the greatest treasure" for the Japanese. This constitution was instituted in the sixth century by Prince Shotoku, a brilliant statesman, who is known and well respected for his adherence to traditional Japanese values, such as social harmony and cooperation. Through the centuries, a consistent theme in Japanese society has been to place strong emphasis on the concept of *wa,* or harmony. Most Japanese to this day adhere to this ideal of smooth relations and avoidance of conflict.

Today, harmony remains the most highly valued and sought after of group mores that company managers in Japan aspire toward. If you visit the office of the president of any Japanese company, or the home of anyone with high social standing, you are likely to find the word "harmony" in framed calligraphy hanging on the wall. Konosuke Matsushita codified his belief in *wa* in the 1970s as one of the seven major company principles and objectives he built his industrial empire from. Konosuke Matsushita expressed his company's principles and objectives in such terms as (1) spirit of service through industry, (2) spirit of fairness, (3) spirit of harmony and unity, (4) spirit of struggle for the sake of progress, (5) spirit of courtesy and humility, (6) spirit of adjustment and assimilation, and (7) spirit of gratitude, in that order.

Contract Agreements

Whether it is between two large companies or between a landlord and a tenant, Japanese contract agreements generally tend to be much less explicit and lack details compared with similar legal contracts in, say, the United States. In concluding a contract agreement in Japan the parties concerned do spell out major points of issue, of course, but it is generally assumed that the documents need not be overly explicit.

Instead, there is usually a special clause toward the end of the document which says something like "in the event any discrepancies or doubts have arisen out of the execution of this contract, both parties will try to eliminate such discrepancies or doubts through mutual negotiation . . . ," or something to this effect. The assumption is that if a situation changes, or if one side is "breaking the contract agreement," it is time for discussion and readjustment between the parties concerned, rather than litigation and accusations.

It is generally believed that it makes little sense to try to specify all conceivable "ifs"–possible conditions or situations that may occur and over which to agree or disagree, and that emphasis should be on mutual trust, and moral or ethical commitments. In fact,

Japanese abhor contract agreements that are full of details, and believe that the spirit of the agreement is more important than its wording. Thus, the Japanese contract agreement is typically less explicit in its legal terminology.

Conference Leadership

In formal meetings, including those where decisions are made, participating members take turns to express their views, usually by order of seniority, instead of monopolizing the discussion. The leader of the meeting usually refrains from voicing his or her views until after everyone else has had an opportunity to speak. The leader will then either sum up the consensus of the group discussion or present his or her own summary. Professor Shuji Hayashi of Tokyo University comments: ". . . either participants of the meeting read the leader's mind in expressing their views or the leader sums up the feelings of the participants in arriving at conclusions or decisions–by which time everyone in the meeting is in harmony with each other."[12]

Conversation

There are times when the Japanese become very reticent. Many tend to be so when circumstances make them feel like avoiding arguments or confrontation, seeking harmony instead. "Out of the mouth comes evil," they say. Not many Japanese–including businesspeople–have been trained in the art or techniques of dialogue, debate, or even general discussion, partly accounting for the tendency to become reserved easily. Unlike Americans, Japanese are generally not good at isolating conflicts and dealing with them.

On the other hand, those who are seen as argumentative or overly persistent are considered disrespectful to group discipline and tend to be shunned by their peers accordingly. It is usually an unspoken rule that things to be discussed "behind the scenes" should not be brought out into the open in the first place, much less dominated by one person's opinion. Talking carelessly is often labeled as "disorderly" or "inharmonious."

Expression

When talking at all, Japanese people are generally very cautious—at times overly cautious—about social consequences, so much so that they tend to express their feelings indirectly, and often resort to vague, indirect speech for protection. This is particularly true among those who have grown up in a predominantly hierarchical society such as Japan's, and is reflected in Japanese business organizations.

Indirect speech is generally understood and accepted among Japanese, who are raised with a propensity for "reading between the lines," but such indirect communication is often a source of misunderstanding between Japanese and foreigners, who may be looking for the speaker's meaning in the words literally.

Along these same lines, Japanese knowingly differentiate between what is known as "tatemae" (official stance or principle; polite language), and "honne" (real intentions or truth). They are known to use lots of "tatemae" rather than "honne" in their speech. People choose one or the other depending on which in their judgement seems to serve the purpose at hand.

Similarly, many Japanese try to soften the tone of speech when declining or when expressing something negative. For example, instead of saying a flat "no," some Japanese feel more comfortable saying "it may be difficult," "I will get back to you later," "maybe," "I wish I could say yes," or perhaps, "I don't know." Others may become speechless and just grin back or bring up a totally different subject. All of this is taken as a harmony-oriented gesture of "no" among Japanese. And on meeting this gesture, the other party is not supposed to push. People know that when harmony is extended, it must be responded to in the same harmonious spirit. This is another trap foreigners often fall into when negotiating with Japanese. The Japanese is not trying to be evasive; he or she is trying to be polite.

Evaluation

The Japanese, businesspeople included, do not like to differentiate between individuals. They feel uncomfortable in distinguishing between good and bad performers, and between capable and incapable workers. This is why American baseball players who join Japanese teams sometimes complain that they are not allowed to play "full-out," and that they are held back from outperforming other players. There is group pressure to "fit in" and preserve the harmonious ties among the members of the team. What's more, individual Japanese often dislike being labeled good or bad. Both good and bad performers are fearful that such ratings may hamper harmony to the detriment of everyone concerned. This feeling is strongly reflected in the Japanese system of employee evaluation and compensation.

INTERPERSONAL RELATIONSHIPS

As this chapter on group orientation emphasizes, most Japanese place maximum value on interpersonal relationships. This value on a personal, individual level is a key link to understanding how Japanese management works. For most Japanese, living and working with others in friendly, cooperative, and coprospering terms is a way of life. Many people make efforts to be modest, humble, kind, and considerate toward others, and look to extend a helping hand to those who need them. But for most Japanese, individual social awareness goes beyond good intentions. Social harmony is so important to Japanese that they are almost always mindful of other peoples' eyes–of what others think of them, and of what the social consequences of various possible actions or words might be, not just for the individual, but for the group. Wherever "enryo" (modesty) and other traditional social protocol is expected, most Japanese will not hesitate to observe it (see *"Enryo"-Driven Workers,* p. 34*).*

These cultural tendencies become all the more pronounced among persons who are close or who are members of the same group–neighbors, colleagues, etc. Professor Gregory Clark of Sophia University, writing in *The Japanese Tribe: Origins of a Nation's Uniqueness,* has described relationships in Japan as concentric. He says:

> The Japanese conceive of themselves as akin to an onion covered by layers of relationships progressively farther from the

core. The closest and most intimate layer consists of family and relatives, and then neighbors, classmates, and colleagues. At the most distant layer are persons with whom one shares nothing in common in terms of birthplace, education or job; such persons are only a thin line from being as distant as foreigners. The Japanese refer to such persons as *tanin* or "other people," that is, outsiders, and such persons may easily be excluded from conscious consideration. The treatment of "other people" as outsiders becomes readily apparent in observations of the interactions of Japanese in formal situations.[13]

In the business world, too, the Japanese place great importance on interpersonal relations. For one thing, in Japan business is done often on the basis of human relations networks or personal "ties"; success or failure of one's business depends a great deal on what personal connections he or she may have. Thus every businessperson tries to establish new "ties" and maintain them.

As members of an organization, too, Japanese exert a lot of effort to getting along well with others, especially in building and upholding good, intimate relations with people around them at work. This is true both internally with senior, junior, and peer-level staff in the same company, and externally with customers, government offices, and the like. Yoshio Hatakeyama, one of the foremost consultants in Japan specializing in management development, urges:

> [The] manager must be able to distribute his energies in a balanced way and mobilize not only his own workers, but also his superiors, his colleagues, and those outside his organization. This is why today's manager is more than simply a high-ranking agent of the company owner; it is as if his section were a company on its own, and he the president.[14]

It is little wonder that many Japanese businesspersons pay meticulous attention to habits such as greetings, entertainment, gifts, and the like.[14]

Hatakeyama thinks that one of the important yardsticks used to determine a manager's promotability to a higher-level position is the ability to deal with people, to establish trust between the manager and the worker, and to motivate and develop the worker.

Other practices or examples that reflect this emphasis on interpersonal relations are as follows.

Personal Introduction

When seeking an appointment with a person one has not met before, far better results can be obtained if he or she is initially introduced through a third party. This personal introduction implies that the person being introduced is someone's "insider" who can be trusted. Thus, Japanese often make the most of their connections in approaching new individuals or organizations. Such connections range from banks, to university professors, to family friends, and others.

Formalities to Maintain Relations

Once initial contacts have been established, people make a point of maintaining such relations more or less on a long-term basis, and observe certain formalities at appropriate occasions, such as entertainments and gift-giving (including calendars, diaries, and other seasonal gifts, either mid-summer or year-end, or both). Frequent visits or phone calls are also accepted as an expression of interest to maintain long-lasting relationships–personally or businesswise, or both.

"Enryo"-Driven Workers

Japanese businesspersons at times are driven to behave out of "enryo" (modesty) or sympathy toward others rather than acting in their own interests. Many feel uneasy not to do so. For example, in taking leave time when their colleagues or bosses appear to be extremely busy, they simply cannot help but feel uncomfortable for not caring about them. Statistics show that the average Japanese working in big companies only take 7.5 days of paid leave a year out of the 15 days authorized.

Paternalistic "Kacho"

Within Japanese organizations which are more or less hierarchical, group members tend to look to their group leaders as good caretakers–like fathers. Managers ranging from "kacho" (section managers), to "bucho" (department managers), up to the president, are all expected to demonstrate some degree of paternalism (see Photo 1.5). This expectation is particularly high of "kacho" to whom a number of the rank and file report day after day. Often the "kacho" is expected to take care of his subordinates over and beyond their official work hours and outside their official workplace–to be a matchmaker, for example. In order to repay the favor thus extended, the subordinates will do their utmost formally or informally.

The "Uchi-Soto" Viewpoint

As Professor Clark pointed out, Japanese tend to look at other people simply from the point of view of whether they belong to

PHOTO 1.5. "Nomi-nication"–drinking communication exchange (nomu means "to drink" in Japanese)–is a widely used technique for demonstration of paternalism as well as communication between a boss and subordinates. *(Courtesy of Japan Management Association)*

"our group" or not. Those who are or appear to belong to "our group," or "uchi" (inner circle), make people feel comfortable to be with them, while those who are conceived of as nonmembers of "our group," or "soto" (outer circle), make people feel uneasy, uncomfortable, and even suspicious. A person's attitude toward the former tends to be warm, friendly, and considerate. The social attitude toward an outsider is cold, unfriendly, and inconsiderate, sometimes even antagonistic.

Anyone can become "uchi," however, depending on common ground, such as shared living environment (geographical proximity), educational background (same school, teachers, subjects, etc.), and working experience (same company, profession, professional memberships). Once the "uchi" attitude is established, it tends to remain alive in the members' minds almost forever, and it acts as a strong bond. The following excerpt from Eizaburo Nishibori's essay serves as a case in point:

> In the traditional mercantile families of Japan, both clerks and apprentices were considered members of the immediate family, and the master's wife handled all matters of room and board and advised them on personal matters as well. . . . My family was originally such a merchant family, and when people who used to work for us would come from the old hometown to visit in later years, we would always put them up and look after them for as much as a week or ten days at a time. We had a very strong sense of their being family members.[15]

Employee Relations

Japanese companies promote strong employee relations, foster closer interpersonal relations, and nurture a sense of shared fortunes among workers. Many, for example, sponsor sports meets for employees and their families, as well as company pleasure trips, farewell parties for employees being relocated elsewhere, welcoming parties for new employees, and year-end parties.

Consumer Networking

Critics agree that Shiseido, one of the most successful cosmetics companies in Japan, has been a classic example of a company achieving tremendous success by extending its clientele relations into organizing a nationwide consumer membership union–in this case, "Hanatsubaki-kai." Similarly, some department stores organize their own customer membership systems to expand sales through closer relations with member customers, for example, the Sezon Club of Seibu Department Store.

RELATED TRENDS AND PERSPECTIVES

The group orientation of the Japanese people will remain unchanged as one of the fundamental Japanese values. For most Japanese, it will be painful to be alone and independent from other people. The majority will continue to want to belong to one group or another, taking part in one group activity or another wherever possible. No one will deny the importance of group harmony.

At the same time, there are some Japanese who are beginning to question the traditional value of blind "groupism." They question, for example, that hardworking Japanese may tend to make too much sacrifice in their own lives in order to serve collective goals of the organizations they work for. They suspect, too, that obsession with the idea of contributing something to the well-being of one's groups may have triggered some individuals to commit wrongdoing such as offering or taking bribes.

On the company level, too, group orientation will basically continue, although business practices based on this value orientation have been challenged dramatically in recent years. The following are examples of these challenges.

Lifetime Employment on the Wane

This time-honored practice is deeply entrenched in Japanese business practice. NEC Corporation of Tokyo reported that as of 1990 all of its staff–literally 100 percent of the employees on the company payroll–were "lifetime employees." But this long-standing tradition in large companies in Japan is now becoming a subject of controversy. Those who are against this tradition of employment point out the drawback of not hiring mid-term employees, as they would contribute valuable experience from outside the company. This, in turn, can keep a company from launching new businesses as quickly as it could otherwise.

Other points being raised by opponents of lifetime employment include the possibility of the employee age structure getting out of balance due to the restrictions on hiring mid-term recruits. There is also the possibility of the traditional system resulting in an excess number of employees on the payroll, and the fear that existing members of an organization may resist newly hired personnel being assigned to positions of high command due to the lack of experience with the hiring of mid-termers.

While some companies are promoting a system of "selective retirement," "early retirement," or "re-employment," to remedy the problem, others are experimenting with nontraditional employment practices such as hiring mid-term workers.

Enthusiastic employees, on their part, are now interested in seeking stimulus for developing personal career goals beyond the restrictions of long-term employment within a particular company. When Yamaha Corporation, one of Japan's major sporting goods manufacturers, offered special benefits to employees if they accepted early retirements, they were shocked to find that as many as 710 workers, or more than 5.5 percent of the total workforce, indicated their willingness to accept the company offer. Of these 710 workers, 100 were middle managers including "kachos" and "buchos."

This ongoing change in traditional lifetime employment practice is reflected in an increase of mid-term hires, too. The results of one private survey indicate that the rate of turnover of college graduates in Japan jumped from about 7 percent in the mid-1980s to about 10 percent by the end of the decade, suggesting that one out of ten college graduates left their first employer within four years of being hired. Employers, meanwhile, have been active in hiring mid-termers, with Seiko-Epson, for example, employing as many as 100 in the year 1987.

Seniority System Under Pressure

One traditional management practice is now also seriously being reviewed. The conventional system of promoting or paying employees on the basis of his or her age or length of service with the employer is fast losing popularity. In its place more and more Japanese want promotions and pay raises based on their work performance.

As to how much of such meritorious factors should be taken into account, opinions differ. For example, Matsushita Electric bases 70 percent of its salaries on individual merit. Interestingly, there are indications that even young employees do not like the idea of being evaluated solely on the basis of merit. Some fear that such an "up or out" evaluation will invite unnecessary competition among employees.

Such mixed opinions notwithstanding, Japanese organizations as a whole will be certain to move toward "evaluating and compensating on the basis of individual merits and contributions," more than ever before. Clearly the seniority-based human resources system is becoming a thing of the past.

The above is not to imply, however, that the Japanese practice of lifetime employment and seniority payment will change drastically in the near future. Both practices will doubtless continue, at least in a limited way. One insurance company is reported to have instituted a system whereby those employees who have preference in a particular area of work–in other words, those who do not like being transferred within the company–may stay permanently "with limited geographical assignment preference." This suggests that certain companies are responding quickly to the changing values of the workforce in terms of human resource employment practice.

Loyalty–A Thing of the Past?

With lifetime employees from within on the decrease and mid-termers from the outside on the increase, there is a fear now that employees' feeling of loyalty–the so-called "company patriotism"–will be lessened more than ever, resulting in the possibility of new management challenges altogether. Japanese workers' sense of belonging will remain strong. Yet just as union membership is losing popularity, so could employees' feelings of loyalty to the company begin to fade away in the coming years–especially in large companies.

In fact, a recent survey reports that the larger the organization is, the less feeling of togetherness there is in the employees' mind. On the question of "work vs. home," many Japanese are still work-oriented, although there are indications that employees favor more of a balance between work and home now than in the past. Under the circumstances, companies will have to proceed with a two-tier system–one for "company loyal" employees and one for "profession loyal" employees.

The Japanese sense of participation and group membership will likely remain unchanged. Both men and women workers will no doubt continue to prefer working in group situations and spending leisure time in group activities. However, with the changes indicated above, it is possible that the overall feeling of participation in each group may eventually become diluted. Individualism, more career orientation, and a desire for more personal time with family and hobbies could weaken feelings of belonging and loyalty within groups. Some factory managers are reported fearful that members of their long-institutionalized small groups may even lose interest in such an affiliation and prefer to become nonmembers.

The practice of small group activities remains popular in Japan, with some 20 million workers estimated as participating in small group activities of one kind or another–approximately one-third of Japan's total workforce.

Management continues to welcome this small group activity system, and they are proud of receiving a good number of employee suggestions. Workers see it as an opportunity to share in a team effort with other employees, and to enlarge their scope of work–which is a source of pleasure for them.

Some Japanese companies are successfully implementing similar approaches in their overseas plants as well, with the same objective of encouraging worker participation. Honda of Ohio, for example, put into practice what they call Voluntary Involvement Program, or VIP, to foster employee participation through employee suggestions and other activities.

Wa (harmony) is and will remain important for the Japanese. Be that as it may, there is criticism about overemphasizing it because it may be used as an excuse for making people reticent or encouraging compromise seekers merely for the sake of keeping harmony. It is possible that the mere emphasis on *wa* alone may not prove very realistic. It may help deprive the Japanese of their tolerance to accommodate people with different perspectives.

Japanese interpersonal relations by and large have been a product of cooperation, with individuals concerned trying to establish relations of mutual interest. These relations are developed over very long periods of time, with particular attention paid to various means of expressions–words and gestures–on the part of both parties. Ideally, relationships developed this way last a lifetime.

The value that the Japanese attach to such interpersonal relations will remain basically unchanged. Individual networks will continue to be important in Japanese business, as well the concept that interpersonal relationships bring about business relationships. Frequent contact and visits with people are and will be important–perhaps more so than anywhere else in the world–whether by telephone, facsimile, face-to-face meetings, "power lunches," or whatever.

One thing that is likely to change, however, is the nature of building business relationships. Japanese will want to build interpersonal relations more on the basis of open, direct, and clear-cut expressions of ideas, instead of on the old style of indirect communication and second-guessing among associates. More and more Japanese are realizing that depending on telepathy does not work in the international arena, and is generally not as efficient as direct communication. Instead, establishing relations with easy-to-understand language is being given more priority than ever. This applies not only with non-Japanese but among Japanese people as well. Gone are the days when modesty was a virtue in business. No longer will the traditional mores and formality-based interpersonal relations take precedence over quick, direct, clear communication.

Chie Nakane's observation that Japanese society is a "vertical society" is well known, yet indications are that another trend is emerging which shows that "horizontal" relations are gaining prevalence. Young Japanese, for example, tend to seek and respect relations with individuals such as former classmates rather than colleagues of the same company. Reports reveal that some families are viewing their parent-child relations more from the standpoint of comrades, and deriving additional delight out of this seemingly new way of relating. Many more women are spending time away from home and developing a number of new relationships with other people.

The Japanese habit of distinguishing between "uchi" (insiders) and "soto" (outsiders) is also here to stay, albeit perhaps in a more sophisticated way than in the past. "Uchi" orientation, for example, which is already strong among those who share the same interests, will possibly become stronger as they grow more profit- and bene-fit-minded over the years. In order to protect their market share, certain interest groups–such as specific industry or local store clus-ters collaborating to keep newcomers out, will continue to be very exclusive and cutthroat. Yet, when the economy is thriving, the same groups may accept newcomers as "uchi" members.

Potential for increased business is also a frequent motivation for opening the door to outsiders. At the work site, some bosses will continue to be very particular about "uchi/soto" distinction, while others may differentiate between the two depending on whom they are dealing with and the specific situation. It is hoped, after all, that all these changes now taking place will result in more flexible, versatile relations among previously exclusive groups, and with outsiders as well.

REFERENCE NOTES

1. Arthur M. Whitehill, 1991. *Japanese Management, Tradition and Transi-tion.* London: Routledge, p. 52.

2. Robert M. March, 1989. *The Japanese Negotiator.* Tokyo: Kodansha In-ternational, pp. 153-154.

3. Sen Nishiyama, 1991. *Shin Gokai to Rikai (Understanding and Misunder-standing).* New edition. Tokyo: The Simul Press.

4. Nihon Keizai Shimbunsha, 1992. *How Different Are Japanese and Ameri-can Corporate Management?* pp. 180-181.

5. Bungei Shunju, *Nippon-teki Keiei ga Abunai (Japanese Management in Crisis),* p. 103.

6. Nippon Research Center, 1992. Market Yoken (Market Projections): *From Euphoria Syndrome to a Sane Society.* Tokyo: Nippon Research Center, Decem-ber.

7. Akio Morita and Shintaro Ishihara, 1989. *"No" to Ieru Nippon (The Japan That Can Say " No")*. Tokyo: Kobunsha.

8. Eizaburo Nishibori, 1985. Nihonjin wa Naze Yoku Hatarakunoka (Why Do the Japanese Work so Hard?), in *Nihon Rashisa (Japanese Essences)*. Tokyo: Kodansha, pp. 132-133.

9. Naomi Yamaki, 1980. *Nihon No Manejimento (Japanese Management)*. Tokyo: Japan Management Association, pp. 176-177.

10. Morimasa Ogawa, 1991. *Pana Management*. Kyoto: PHP Institute, Inc.

11. Sadaharu Sato, 1992. *Gekido Ni Ikiru Keieisha Kanrisha (Executives and Managers Who Survive in Times of Turbulence)*. Fukuoka: Shudan-Rikigaku Kenkyusho, pp. 74-78.

12. Shuji Hayashi, 1984. *Keiei to Bunka (Culture and Management in Japan)*. Tokyo: Chuo Koron Sha, p. 118.

13. Gregory Clark, 1977. *The Japanese Tribe: Origins of a Nation's Uniqueness* (The Japanese translation: *Nipponjin: Yunikusa no Gensen*, by Masumi Muramatsu). Tokyo: The Simul Press.

14. Yoshio Hatakeyama, 1985. *Manager Revolution!* Productivity Press, Stamford, CN, p. 5.

15. Eizaburo Nishibori, 1985. "Nihonjin wa Naze Yoku Hatarakunoka" ("Why do the Japanese Work so Hard?"), in *Nihon Rashisa (Japanese Essences)*. Tokyo: Kodansha.

Chapter 2

Diligence

THIRST FOR KNOWLEDGE

Pursue learning with full speed lest you be far behind it, however fast you may run.

Industry is fortune's right hand and frugality her left.

One should not bequeath bountiful rice paddies to one's offspring.

The Japanese, in general, place much value on learning. Learning has been a virtue throughout the history of Japan. It is said that Francisco Xavier, upon his visit to Japan in the sixteenth century as a missionary, observed that the Japanese were a people with a keen appetite for knowledge.

Japanese parents are dedicated to educating their children, so much so that children are taught to study in their infancy. History has it that during the Edo Period (seventeenth to nineteenth century), enthusiastic parents throughout the country worked together voluntarily to open private schools called "terakoya" (temple schools) in their village temples and other public places. As a consequence, children of five years of age and over had some opportunity to learn to read and write and use the "soroban" (abacus) as a means of calculation. The high rate of literacy, of which the Japanese people are proud, is rooted in the "terakoya" education of 200 to 300 years ago.

Today, a number of Japanese students go to high schools and then to universities or other institutions of higher learning. In fact, a university degree is considered to be a minimum requirement for anyone to achieve success in life. Thus, a growing number of high school students exert extraordinary efforts to enter into universities each year. The latest statistics show that as much as 39 percent of all high school students go on to receive university educations.[1]

Many Japanese will not cease to pursue learning even after joining a company upon graduation. Among other things, they insist on studying different aspects of a job–even human relations in the workplace. Employers are in most cases willing to help them pursue self-improvement, with many companies sponsoring their own educational programs for their employees, ranging from on-the-job training to overseas study tours and enrollment in overseas colleges and universities.

In short, for the majority of Japanese workers, companies are places both for work and study–at least in their expectations. The late Konosuke Matsushita once stated that "Matsushita makes people before it makes electric appliances." Today, Japanese companies, on average, are expending about one-tenth of a percent of total company sales volume for employee training and education.

THE JAPANESE WORK ETHIC

The Japanese work hard. Most of them honestly like to work. They see their jobs as their foremost source of meaning of life. To be called a diligent worker is the highest form of praise in Japan.

Among the Japanese, "he or she is a hard worker" denotes a person who is dedicated to a task conscientiously and single-mindedly despite certain difficulties or temptations. Japanese place high value on someone who approaches a job persistently and wholeheartedly and who devotes long and untiring hours for its successful completion. Many Japanese try to become such a worker, but often without success, and therefore end up simply admiring those who have achieved a high level of diligence and success.

Why do the Japanese work so hard? Most Japanese believe there are at least three principal reasons.

One, the tradition of rice-paddy culture demands a heavy concentration of labor for relatively short periods several times each year. Industriousness is required to avoid any delay in planting or harvesting that might result from adverse weather conditions.

Two, the Japanese have a long history of economic deprivation. Extremely poor living conditions made it absolutely necessary for the Japanese to work hard to ensure their survival.

Three, Confucian thought, which reached Japan during the sixth century, held up frugality and diligence as moral virtues. It taught, among other things, that work was good and play was bad. Idleness was shameful and immoral.

Many Japanese work just as hard–or even harder–when working as a member of group. Former Ambassador to Japan and renowned Japanese scholar Edwin O. Reischauer has written: "The (Japanese) work ethic . . . has probably been strengthened rather than weakened by the group orientation of the Japanese. A good group cooperator is also a good worker."[2]

Professor Toyoyuki Sabata of Kyoto Prefectural University of Medicine has a similar view. He says, "Japanese diligence is manifested most effectively in a family-type atmosphere. It is for this reason that the Japanese worked so hard to create a family-like atmosphere in their drive for modernization . . . such corporate traits as lifetime employment and seniority wage systems are products of this orientation."[3]

In the business world, too, the Japanese are indisputably a hard-working people (see Figure 2.1). Many devote long hours to their jobs. Most people working in business have one thing in common– addiction to getting the job done. As indicated below, what drives them to work so hard varies.

A "Work is Life" Attitude

A number of Japanese people find inherent worth in labor itself. Many work by the sweat of their brow just to have a meaningful life, and many continue to work after retirement (which is at age sixty). There are those, too, who see work in Buddhist terms as a form of spiritual discipline, requisite to achieving Nirvana.

Success and Fame

Many Japanese pursue their dream to attain a high position in an organization or high status in society. Most of the successful senior

FIGURE 2.1. Annual Hours Worked by Manufacturing/Industry Workers (Estimates for 1990)

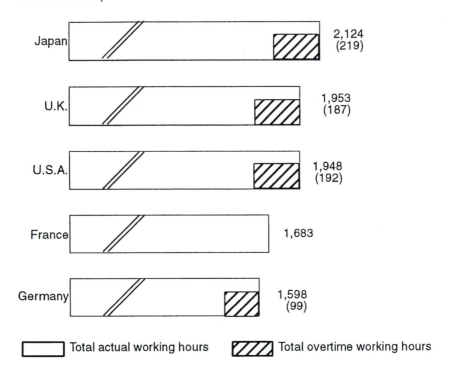

Note: Company scale: those with five employees or more (Japan), all companies (U.S.), and those with ten employees or more (others).

Source: Nippon, *Business Facts & Figures* 1993, JETRO.

executives of Japanese organizations are those who have climbed up the organization ladder by means of hard work and long years of service, rather than being invited from the outside. This fact is well known in Japan, and serves to inspire people in lower positions to work hard.

Economic Incentives

For many Japanese, economic incentives constitute one of the biggest factors in their desire to work. In a government survey in

1992, more than half of Japanese polled said they could not afford to live without their incomes.

Competition

Some Japanese businesspersons are driven to work by a sense of competition with others, whether other individuals, companies, or nations. As an organization is always engaged in fierce competition with external rivals, its staff members are called on to exert themselves to meet the competition goals, either as a team or individually.

Typhoon Mentality

When facing hardships, such as typhoons, earthquakes, and the like, the Japanese tend to exert extraordinary efforts to recover from such calamities quickly. The post-World War II economic rehabilitation is one such example, and the recovery from the two oil crises during the 1970s was another. Eizaburo Nishibori (see p. 41) supports this view: "... working in collaboration is the reason why the Japanese work so well."[4]

Nevertheless, even Japanese who take great pleasure in their jobs may at times lose the incentive to work. Generally this happens when they feel they are being "compelled" to work by someone else, or when they feel they are not being entrusted with tasks that demand individual responsibility.

For example, during the years of the American Occupation after World War II, Japanese laborers in charge of snow removal at American military bases got angry and loafed on the job because the American soldiers who gave them their orders refused to grant them occasional breaks during the day for a cigarette–a deeply ingrained habit among Japanese workers. Without doubt the Japanese laborers would have performed their jobs assiduously if only the Americans had just indicated the results they expected and left actual work methods–including the freedom to take cigarette breaks–to the Japanese themselves.

The same argument is heard among Japanese staff working in multinational corporations in Japan. In their opinion, more effective results would surely be achieved if development and marketing of products for the Japanese market were left to the Japanese staff, who are familiar with their home market, rather than attempting simply to force non-Japanese marketing techniques or products onto the Japanese consumer.

The Japanese willpower to work can be lessened, too, if there are fruits that may be harvested without toil. An old Japanese adage that states that one should not bequeath bountiful rice paddies to one's offspring is meant to suggest that although leaving bountiful paddies to one's progeny would certainly be to their immediate benefit, it might ultimately have the negative effect of slanting their individual will to work.

GAMBARISM–HANG IN THERE!

The Japanese language contains a frequently used verb, gambaru, which roughly translates as, "Hang in there" or "Keep trying." Gambaru implies exerting great energy or emotional vehemence, thought, or action to accomplish an objective, particularly in the face of adversity. In real life, the Japanese gambaru in many ways.

A typical example of the Japanese gambaru spirit–or gambarism–is found in Tokyo's famed morning rush hour (see Photo 2.1). In the eyes of most foreigners, the fierce crowding and resultant pushing and shoving that are inevitable features of the early morning routine in big cities are nothing short of insanity. And yet, this is perhaps gambarism at its best.

Gambarism also runs rampant among students of high school age who are preparing for college entrance examinations. Such students gambaru by sleeping as little as three or four hours each night in a determined effort to do their best. Parents also gambaru by pushing their children to do better at school, in their after-school private lessons, and in their various cultural or educational pastimes.

Japanese gambarism escalates all the more when an individual becomes a member of a group or team. Members of a high school baseball team, for example, will spend day after day practicing to exhaustion to qualify for the semiannual nationwide tournaments in order to win, if fortune smiles on them. The same drive runs through professional baseball. Foreign players recruited to play on Japanese teams are almost invariably stunned, if not appalled, when

PHOTO 2.1. The fierce crowding and resultant pushing and shoving are inevitable features of the early morning rush hours in big cities. *(Courtesy of Japan Management Association)*

they discover just how hard their Japanese teammates gambaru for the sake of the game.

Above all else, however, Japanese gambaru most in the corporate setting. Workers strive for the sake of group goals–to attain, for example, planned sales goals or productivity targets by a specified date. Managers keep workers under pressure requiring them to make improvements wherever possible. They would urge: "If money is not available, use your head. If your head is not available, work by the sweat of your brow."[5]

Critics say that the general Japanese proclivity toward gambarism in the corporate environment has become pronounced particularly since the end of World War II. After the war, labor unions waged fierce battles in their effort to improve labor conditions, and through strikes and other tactics they succeeded in creating havoc for management. Yet as a result Japan–both management and employees–grew accustomed to a never-ending pursuit of the rationalization of operations. In any case, the tradition of gambarism remains alive in many Japanese companies today as a value of pivotal significance.

RELATED TRENDS AND PERSPECTIVES

Most Japanese are likely to continue to put great effort into their studies; nothing will stop their appetite for knowledge.

Somewhat pessimistic views are emerging, however, regarding the Japanese attitude toward hard work. As their society grows affluent, they say, the traditional value placed on industriousness will diminish. Observers point to the seeming decline in the will to work on the part of Japanese workers, especially among young people. Professor Kunio Odaka of Tokyo University shares this view. He writes, "Our work ethic has been worm-eaten."[6]

On the other hand, there are those who believe that work will remain the central concern of life for most Japanese, and the author is inclined to support this view. The traditional consciousness of hard work has been so deeply ingrained in the minds of the Japanese that it is difficult for them to assume that such a value orientation will ever change dramatically; nor can they see that the Japanese will ever cease to be motivated by those driving forces mentioned earlier in this chapter, including the element of economic incentives.

While the Japanese work ethic is and will continue to be more pervasive and more widely accepted throughout its society compared to other countries, there is one thing that is coming under increasing criticism both from within and outside of Japan of late; and that is the way they spend their time at work.

Why, for example, are Japanese so unconcerned about taking–or, rather, not taking–more days or time off work and using such time with their families or for their personal interests over a period of a year? The fact is, many salaried workers do not even take two full days off every weekend; and that is in addition to taking only half of their accrued annual leave which averages 16 days a year across the board. Further, the number of days of absence from work hardly compares with that of workers from other countries.

Also coming under scrutiny is the matter of efficiency. Traditionally, Japanese have tended to devote a bit too much time to getting a job done. Long hours of work, or single-minded devotion of time, was considered a virtue and praiseworthy. Thus people are used to spending much time doing things individually or as a group–sometimes an inordinate length of time by Western standards. As a result, either bosses or subordinates, or both, tend to expect workers to spend extra hours to get necessary work done. Efficiency, therefore, often becomes secondary to putting in long hours. In 1990 the Japanese industrial worker worked 219 overtime hours on average–some 120 hours longer than their German counterparts, and between 27 and 32 hours longer than their U.S. and U.K. counterparts.[7]

Gambarism, too, is likely to stay with the Japanese business community. Most Japanese believe that to gambaru, or to hang in there, is meritorious.

This does not mean that gambarism is without problems, however. For example, people tend to hold the gambaru "process" in high esteem. To gambaru in itself is of the utmost importance, the actual result being only secondary. For students and baseball players alike, it is those who gambaru who are praised. Conversely, those who exert no gambarism receive little praise, even if they produce favorable results without it.

Related to this focus on the gambaru "process," Japanese tend to sacrifice time–another important resource people have–by working overtime, giving up vacation or accrued leave days with pay, or just devoting more time to work than necessary, etc. For example, some work from seven in the morning through eleven at night and are called, jokingly, "Seven-eleven men." Thus, gambarism competition can develop among members of a group with everyone competing for extra hard work, and the extra praise or reward that comes with it.

Gambarism is also subject to a somewhat different and not necessarily flattering interpretation. In this view, gambarism, though instilling intense dedication to those things in which one believes, simultaneously rejects common values or value systems that lie outside this personal frame of judgement. Consider, for example, how a hurried (and selfish) Japanese will force his or her way onto a densely crowded train, ultimately delaying its departure. Or consider how Company X might reduce the price of its product in an effort to sell it at any cost, even though such action might well generate turmoil in the marketplace.

REFERENCE NOTES

1. Nippon, 1993. JETRO *Business Facts and Figures*.
2. Edwin O. Reischauer, 1983. *The Japanese*. Tokyo: Charles E. Tuttle Company, p. 154.
3. Toyoyuki Sabata, 1985. "Komezukuri ni Nezashita Nihon No Bunka" ("The Rice-Cultivation-Oriented Culture of Japan"), in *Nihon Bunka O Saguru (Behind Japanese Culture)*. Tokyo: Kodansha, pp. 88-89.
4. Eizaburo Nishibori, 1985. "Nihonjin wa Naze Yoku Hatarakunoka" ("Why do the Japanese work so hard"), in *Nihon Rashisa (Japanese Essences)*. Tokyo: Kodansha, pp. 132-133.
5. Masaaki Imai, 1988. *Kaizen (Improvement)*. Tokyo: Kobunsha.
6. Kunio Odaka, 1988. *Nihonteki Keiei (Japanese-Style Management)*. Tokyo: Chuokoronsha.
7. Nippon, 1983. JETRO *Business Facts and Figures*.

Chapter 3

Aesthetics and Perfectionism

THE JAPANESE SENSE OF AESTHETICS

Different people have different senses of, and attach varying levels of importance to, beauty. The Japanese sense of aesthetics, first and foremost, involves nature itself, that is, the appreciation of nature's changes. They enjoy cherry blossoms in the spring, the moon in the summer, and changing colors of leaves in the autumn. In fact, their joy from viewing such changes is so great it sometimes induces them to write songs and poetry to express it. There are also those who find pleasure in simulating nature to have an appreciation of nature–its beauty, its grace, its simplicity, and its serenity. Japanese gardens, "bonsai" (potted miniature trees), and "tokonoma" (an alcove provided in a Japanese guest room), all reflect the Japanese love of nature. Japan's famed flower arrangement and tea ceremony are other examples.

In his book, *Culture and Management in Japan*, Professor Shuji Hayashi of Shizuoka University describes how Japanese feel about nature, especially in contrast with Chinese and Korean perceptions:

Sen no Rikyu (1522-1591) was tea master to the leaders Oda Nobunaga and Toyotomi Hideyoshi and founder of the Sen school of tea ceremony. One bright autumn day, having invited guests for a tea ceremony, he ordered a young monk to clean the small temple garden. The monk swept up every fallen leaf and told Rikyu that the job was finished. The tea master glanced at the scene and stepped down into the garden. He gently shook two or three trees until a few dead leaves fell to the ground. "Now the stage is set for our guests," he said.

A south Korean intellectual has criticized this incident as typical Japanese affectation. He said that a Chinese would probably have left the garden clear of leaves, as the priest had cleaned it, and a Korean would have held the ceremony with all the fallen leaves just as they were, in their natural state, finding that truly beautiful.[1]

Japanese seek and enjoy beauty not only in their dealings with nature but with material objects that people may happen to have in their possession. For example, they are tempted to admire the materials, designs, patterns, colors, finishes, etc., that may have been used in one's houses, rooms, furniture, etc., as well as in potteries, ceramics, and other wares or clothes that may have been put to use in one's everyday life. Many also feel comfortable with the "tatami" (straw mat) floor, partly due to its color and cushion, but partly due to the smell it generates which resembles nature.

As well, Japanese in general are fond of preparing and eating food in as attractive a manner as possible (see Photo 3.1). A supreme example is the *Maku-no-uchi* style boxed lunch. This typically contains small portions each of rice, cooked dishes, grilled items, pickled vegetables, and so on. Although the ingredients themselves may be quite mundane, they are placed into the lacquered container in a way to create a meal of great visual beauty. The partaker of the meal derives as much pleasure from this beautifully arranged meal as its preparer.

The Japanese demonstrate delicate sensitivity toward other people, too, which is also a manifestation of their aesthetic sense, according to Professor Chuichi Kitagawa of Joban University. For example, when eating a meal or after finishing it, many Japanese will take precautions to maintain a neat appearance around the table in order to avoid giving unpleasant impressions to others nearby. For example, when eating a mandarin orange, many Japanese will remove the peel in one, unbroken piece, and place segment membranes inside the outer peel, so that the leftover materials end up in a neatly wrapped little package. When one finishes a meal, he or she will set chopsticks down on the table neatly aligned again to keep the table looking pleasant.

As in the West, in Japanese restaurants it is fairly common to

PHOTO 3.1. Japanese are fond of preparing and eating food in as attractive a manner as possible. *(Courtesy of Japan Management Association)*

place the check face down on the customer's table so that the cost of the meal may not be seen until the customer has finished eating and is ready to pay.

Japanese custom has it that when one receives a gift, he or she is not expected to unwrap it just in case it may embarrass either the giver or the receiver, or both, for one reason or another. If the situation makes it desirable for the receiver to unwrap the gift, he or she will do so carefully, keeping the wrapping paper in a hypothetically reusable condition before admiring the gift. This derives from a concern for appearance as well as an expression of gratitude to the giver. Treating the wrapping paper carelessly may in some cases even be taken as a gesture of displeasure with the contents of the present.

When tipping a maid in a Japanese hotel for some extra service offered–one of few occasions tipping ever takes place in Japan–sensible customers would wrap the money in a piece of paper or put it in a tiny envelope before handing it over to the maid. The feeling here is that handing the bare cash to someone is not very graceful and therefore should be avoided as much as possible.

In the world of business, too, the Japanese demonstrate aesthetics in a number of ways. Most barbers do an elaborate job in haircutting, rinsing, and massaging. "Kimono" sewers insist on doing their very best in sewing even in those areas which are hidden from outside view. Other examples follow.

Drawings May Be Sent Back

Some workers on the production floor are totally dedicated to the purpose at hand, no matter how menial it may be. Thus, when they find that doing the work as specified in the drawings provided may not yield good results, these workers will not hesitate to bring such drawings back to their bosses or order dispatchers for reconsideration, if not redrawing. For most workers, doing work precisely as specified and subsequently turning out what may prove to be unsatisfactory simply will not dissuade their aesthetic sense.

5S Campaign

For some years now, the "5S campaign" has been prevalent in a number of factories. The term "5S" was derived from the first letter of the five Japanese words starting with S in Roman characters, i.e., seiri (organize the workplace), seiton (keep it neat), seiso (keep it clean), seiketsu (maintain the standardized conditions), and shitsuke (maintain the discipline). The whole idea behind this campaign is to promote the excellent housekeeping within a factory which aesthetically oriented Japanese believe is conducive to the production of quality products as well as the safety and productivity in the workplace.

Work Rather than Time

Professor Hayashi, mentioned above, believes that the Japanese display another sense of aesthetic, that of struggling to complete a task against the clock. In a survey of businesspeople in three countries–Japan, South Korea, and Taiwan–respondents were asked to reply to the following question (paraphrased): "How would you look upon a worker who goes home at the regular quitting time even when the task he is currently working on could be completed by working 30 minutes extra?" Of Korean respondents, 52.7 percent supported the worker's stance; of Taiwanese, 29.7 percent; and of Japanese, only 7.4 percent. In other words, most Japanese feel that rather than adhering to prescribed work hours inflexibly, they would rather stay an extra 30 minutes and complete a task in progress.

"Japanese feel very uncomfortable about leaving a task 90 percent finished," states Professor Hayashi. In other words, leaving a task unfinished runs counter to Japanese aesthetics. South Korean executives, in contrast, do "not like to ignore set work hours and continue at a job in the casual style so common in Japanese offices." In other words, the latter runs counter to Korean aesthetics.

IT MUST BE PERFECT!

"How I wish I could have done more perfect work!" many Japanese would say in reviewing the job just completed. This shows that they value doing things thoroughly to completion; otherwise they tend to be left with a feeling of dissatisfaction.

Japanese affinity for perfectionism is manifested not only in individual activities but in organizational and social activities as well. Individually, Japanese insist on studying all aspects of a question before starting a project or even a new sport or hobby. People concerned with a complex university entrance examination system try to carry it out in a manner approaching near perfection.

Thirst for Mastery

Many Japanese long to become a master or an expert, or near such, in their chosen activity–be it Judo, Ikebana (flower arrangement), Sushi cooking, or anything else–and to achieve this they undergo extensive self-induced training or exercise (see Photo 3.2).

PHOTO 3.2. Many Japanese will spend their free time studying such things as the tea ceremony, flower arrangement, and cooking, etc. Some will undergo extensive training or exercise to become a master or an expert. *(Courtesy of Japan Management Association)*

Company employees are no exception. Most will be enthusiastic in learning new skills and challenging new jobs. Many will strive to become "number one" in a given work or workplace; they will never let some seeming problems ride; they will want to be absolutely sure that whatever they do is perfect.

Attention to Details

For the majority of Japanese, details are quite important. These people dislike being rough and insensitive, with many placing high value upon sensitivity and attentiveness and expecting the same of others. In a TV program on cooking, an expert instructor would specify that *mirin*, or sweetened sake, to be added to certain foods, will have to be no more and no less than "a quarter of a spoonful" rather than just "a little bit" or "a splash."

Zero Defect

Japanese manufacturing companies are fond of setting down objectives that are nearly impossible to attain–and then attempting to attain them. On the production floor, for example, one finds "ZD" or "Zero defect" as a goal to be achieved in parts fabrication or assembly lines.

Listening to the Gods' Voices

Japanese organizations also insist on collecting and then analyzing market information and related data to near perfection. Each company makes a thorough investigation of consumers' needs and wants and tries to produce goods that will reflect such consumers', or gods', voices. Although religious beliefs are not generally associated with this "customer is a god" attitude, it reflects the seriousness with which Japanese regard customer service and satisfaction. Japanese automakers will never hesitate to attach a steering wheel right or left depending on what a particular market, or customer, may dictate.

During the 1940s, Konosuke Matsushita, founder of Matsushita Electric, in launching a campaign to sell the company's high-value-added items, left this message to company employees: "As industrialists, whether in manufacturing or sales, the only way we can truly gain the confidence of customers is to provide them with only quality products which meet their needs in every way . . . we must be perfect in satisfying."[2]

Fastidious Consumers

Japanese consumers are known to be among the most demanding in the world. Not only do they expect goods for sale to be of reputed quality, but they are equally sensitive about the way they are packaged, delivered, and priced, as well as about after-sale services. Should they find anything wrong or not fully satisfying, Japanese consumers will easily go to other shops to find a better or more desirable product or service. Some consumers are even willing to pay top dollar when they find exactly what they want. This relentless demand for quality products and services on the part of the Japanese consumer has a profound impact on the imported items as well as the distribution systems that are involved.

Says Mr. Hideyuki Kameda, General Manager of Kameda Shoji, an electronics parts producer and marketer: " . . . Japan is a zero defect country. The system is so strict that it does not permit even one single defective product out of a million onto the market. . . . Even though a product may be considered to be of high quality abroad, it doesn't necessarily mean that it will be viewed as such in Japan."[3]

Mr. Michiro Kusano, President of a joint venture company selling concrete forming and shoring systems with aluminum equipment, shares a similar view: " . . . The Japanese market is a strict market that demands zero defects . . . without adequate and consistent product quality, it is difficult to get repeat customers. . . . "[4]

RELATED TRENDS AND PERSPECTIVES

The Japanese will continue to cherish their own sense of aesthetics. Many will not cease to admire the beauty of nature, or to attach importance to the particular sensitivities Japanese have in dealing with other people.

Also, just as in the production of traditional crafts in Japan, such as the Kimono, Japanese will continue to insist on producing quality items with what may even seem like unreasonable attention to detail by Westerners. In lacquerware, for example, name lacquerware producers will always be in demand, and preferred by the customer because quality is assured. This is the tradition as it is applied in manufacturing also, and it is not likely that such a deeply ingrained practice will change overnight.

Yet, there are indications that suggest that Japanese ways of demonstrating aesthetics may be changing. For example, while loving beauty and serenity, many urban Japanese are becoming insensitive to trash and litter on the street or noise pollution in the subway. Some even "wash their dirty linen in public," which refers to an unsightly forest of garish "love hotels" springing up adjacent to family residential areas. These distasteful products of modern life are for most Japanese a matter of serious concern.

Report after report confirms that consumers' aesthetic has changed in recent years. Traditionally, people used to be fond of purchasing things that they thought looked pretty or fancy, lovely or cute, sweet or tasteful. Once, almost everyone wanted things that were simply necessary or convenient. But with the abundance of products available in the past few decades, ranging from those goods which looked fairly functional or durable to those reputed to be only fashionable or "foreign made," things began to change.

Yet, today's Japanese consumer is still reported to be more particular or outspoken about healthy, safe foods, and "easy to understand" electronic appliances, for example, as compared to many of the world's consumers. The current direction in Japan is to go more and more for products that have practical value while continuing to keep their traditional aesthetic standards and sensitivities.

Similarly, the Japanese sense of aesthetic is changing with respect to work versus personal free time. As discussed earlier, most Japanese workers have preferred to continue to work on a project until reaching a logical place to stop, even if it meant staying late on the job. But this attitude toward work time is changing. In a private survey of 2,000 salaried workers in metropolitan areas, 57 percent of male respondents said "I will return home when closing time comes," against 53 percent in 1990, and 69 percent of female respondents said the same thing against 65 percent in 1990. The Japanese aesthetic in this respect may continue changing as more young Japanese join the workforce in the future.

Yet, notwithstanding such changes, the Japanese basically will continue to inherit some of the traditional sense of aesthetics, such as the love of nature, passion for quality items, and respect for interpersonal sensitivity.

The Japanese will also seek to be perfectionistic whenever and wherever it appears possible. Sushi cooks in sushi bars will do their best to please their customers as much as workers at auto repair shops will do their repair work thoroughly to completion. At times, such people try to achieve perfection in their jobs even if it is not profitable.

The Japanese propensity for details will doubtless continue. Both individuals and organizations will continue to be fervent collectors of data and information and at the same time ardent readers of such materials. In fact, the Japanese business world is likely to continue to be extremely well informed.

The over-zealous attention to details, however, can make some Japanese blind about a larger world–a you-cannot-see-the-forest-for-the-trees syndrome. Businesspersons who come to learn the Western manners of drinking and eating in a formal situation easily get enthused with the use of dinnerware, etc., and soon forget about other, perhaps more important aspects of drinking or eating–the protocol of conversation with other people, for example.

There are other issues with "perfectionists," which can become even more serious than the above example. One such issue relates to those who tend to be preoccupied with their own interests and move around intensely to accomplish their own objectives, often causing misunderstanding and conflict with other people–particularly those who do not share the same values. As a case in point, Chung Ju Yung, Chairman of the Hyundai Group, South Korea's largest industrial group, is quoted as saying: ". . . They claim that the Hyundai Pony is selling extremely well in Canada. But in fact the Pony accounts for only a ten percent market share. By contrast, Japanese never appear satisfied unless they completely corner every market they enter." Chung goes on to say, "In economics as in war, the best policy is not to seek overwhelming victory. For although this may lead to a temporary victory, there is no true victory in the long run if the defeated party is made to starve."[5]

Another issue with the Japanese admiration for "perfection" has to do with their inability to express themselves as openly as they like in public. The Japanese are known to be a bashful people and to be introspective. Part of this stems from the tendency to pursue perfectionism in expression, either in speaking a foreign language or in dancing at a social party or the like. And knowing that one is far from being "perfect," he or she quickly becomes hesitant even to give it a try–the polar view, perhaps, of the Westerner's "learn by doing" mentality.

All in all, as long as Japanese continue to be as "conscientious" as they have been, this perfectionism is certain to be instilled in many young Japanese now and for generations to come.

REFERENCE NOTES

1. Shuji Hayashi, 1984. *Keiei to Bunka (Culture and Management in Japan)*. Tokyo: Chuo Koron Sha.

2. Jerry Bowles, April 1992. "Is American Management Really Committed to Quality?" *AMA Management Review.*

3. Hideyuki Kameda, 1991. JETRO, The Challenge of the Japanese Market: The Manufacturing Success–Nine Foreign Affiliated Companies with Plants in Japan.

4. Ibid.

5. Chung Ju Yung, 1986. *Soto Kara Mita Nippon (Japan as Seen from Abroad)*, edited by Asahi Shimbun Gaihobu. Tokyo: Asahi Shimbun, p. 210.

Chapter 4

Curiosity and Emphasis on Innovation

Ask and ye shall receive.

Where there's a will, there's a way.

Nothing is so good that it couldn't have been better.

CURIOSITY

History tells us that, dating back to as early as the seventh century, the Japanese have been sending visitors to and receiving visitors from China in order to learn the country's social and cultural systems. Luis Frois, a missionary who visited Japan in the fifteenth century, is said to have commented that "the curiosity of the Japanese is overwhelming." Later, in the seventeenth century, reading, writing, and arithmetic captured the interest of the people, leading to the construction of schools for the general public known as "terakoya" throughout Japan (see Chapter 2, page 45).

The Japanese are always extremely interested in the events taking place around them, and this interest often extends to the smallest detail. This is particularly true in the case of phenomena occurring in foreign countries, whether in an emotional or intellectual context.

According to Sophia University Professor Gregory Clark, the Japanese are far more influenced by events taking place around them than are Americans and Europeans. He adds that "the receptive nature of the Japanese toward outside information derives from the groupism of Japanese society."[1]

Japanese curiosity is particularly keen with respect to those things which are new and different. They exhibit no resistance to these things, and in fact take to them aggressively. As soon as laser disc home video systems were put on the market, they were scooped up for use in households throughout Japan, and this is by no means a rare example. Currently, Japanese homes, and indeed all areas of society at large, exhibit remarkable diversity, including food, clothing, furniture, or even religion (see Photo 4.1).

By and large, businesspeople also have a strong sense of curiosity, and are extremely concerned with the acquisition of information.

Learning from Foreign Countries

Most Japanese businessmen have a never-ending interest in how their counterparts in foreign countries do their work, what types of unique experiences they have, and what results they are consequently achieving. Back when Nissan Motors began building the Austin, Nissan engineers are said to have visited the engineers of the Austin and showered them with questions. Nowadays as well, whether in groups or individually, large numbers of Japanese flock to foreign trade shows to scour for new knowledge with their own eyes and ears, and to explore and evaluate the potential of novel ideas.

Zealous at Work

Japanese businessmen are almost without exception aggressive information mongers, to the extent that they might even be said to be suffering from "information thirst syndrome." They readily work in open offices where discussions and telephone conversations can be freely heard, they readily participate in conferences and meetings, and they readily exchange information as a daily affair whenever time permits. By presenting information in advance, they are able in most cases to garner understanding, approval, and support. Conversely, if they fail to do so, chances are they will be met with indifference and opposition.

Sen Nishiyama, an essayist with business experience which

PHOTO 4.1. Japanese towns today reflect Westernization that has taken place since the nineteenth century. *(Courtesy of Japan Management Association)*

spans the cultural differences between the United States and Japan, recounts the following situation. "In a certain Japanese company, a single American was employed. He was satisfied with his work, and the company was satisfied with his performance. From time to time, however, he attempted to act on an idea by himself, and was then frustrated when things didn't go well. The ideas themselves were good, but many never reached fruition since he neglected to go through proper channels beforehand. Curiously, though, certain other ideas were in fact carried out successfully. Why? Because he happened to discuss these ideas with his Japanese colleagues, and the Japanese employees circulated them among the relevant individuals within the organization. This American may have mentioned his ideas in passing, but probably didn't give it much thought."

To restate, when the Japanese are informed of something, they generally feel as though they have in essence been consulted on it, and as a result have a tendency to readily act on it.

Information-Sharing and Inter-Departmental Cooperation

In Japanese factories, the sharing of information across, for example, design, pilot production, and manufacturing departments, is natural and proper. Osaka University Professor Iwao Nakatani explains. "As a result of this information sharing and coordination, pilot production can begin while design is being carried out and production lines can be built while design changes are being made. Such information feedback among departments concerned makes the development of mass production items in relatively short periods of time possible."[2]

Similarly, when complaints are received from customers or dealers, representatives of relevant departments are assembled in order to perform exhaustive fact finding and data collection. Customers and dealers also are asked to help out by offering a considerable amount of feedback. Some Japanese car manufacturers are encouraging this sort of interdepartmental information sharing in their American subsidiaries, and are receiving favorable reactions from their local staff members.

Dealer Support

At Kao Corporation, a detergent manufacturer, the sharing of information has been extended to include dealers. Specifically, every day from ten in the morning until closing time, the company receives and analyzes point-of-sale data from model stores all over the country and, in turn, sends "The Kao News" out to the homes of employees of Kao dealers by fax twice a week.[3]

EMPHASIS ON INNOVATION

As already mentioned, the Japanese exhibit a fondness for changing things (see The Japanese Sense of Aesthetics, p. 55). Many Japanese tend to get bored with the status quo; whatever the reason, they are just not eternally satisfied with the same old things. Even for things which are traditional or which come from abroad, change is viewed as good, and new is viewed as better than old.

Rebuilding of the Ise Shrine

The Japanese feel no compunctions about rebuilding the Ise Shrine, a symbol of the nation, every 20 years, and in fact feel that this is quite sensible (see Photo 4.2). Statistically, the average lifespan of buildings in Tokyo is only 17 years. In the eyes of the Japanese, buildings both new and old should be renovated, and cities and parkland alike should be rebuilt with the passage of time. As one commentator puts it: "Whether it be the Ise Shrine or an average home, the feeling is that because of the wood construction, renovation is inevitable. There is a common mentality that anything built must ultimately change. This is a view which is not found in cultures formed on stone construction."[4]

Educational Innovation

Following World War II, the Japanese adopted the American 6-3-3 educational system for their own. And yet, despite the magnitude of this switch, the system was accepted without the slightest resistance.

To the Japanese, renovation signifies the birth of things which are more efficient or more acceptable. Consider the following examples.

The Japanese Language

In the seventh century, the Japanese took notice of the Chinese idiographic *(kanji)* characters. They adopted these characters unaltered, transformed some into phonetic *(kana)* characters, and then added this combination to the Japanese language they had been using since the third century. These idiographic and phonetic characters have jointly comprised the Japanese formal writing system ever since.

In similar fashion, the Japanese adopted Portuguese words in the fifteenth century, and introduced English starting in the nineteenth century. In most of these cases the Japanese adopted the original words with their foreign pronunciation rather than translating them into new Japanese equivalents, and in so doing were successful in

PHOTO 4.2. The Japanese people take it for granted that even the Ise Shrine, a symbol of the nation, is rebuilt once every 20 years. To most Japanese, change is good and new is better than old. *(Courtesy of Japan Management Association)*

expanding their vocabulary considerably. The Japanese words "pan" (bread, from Portuguese), "torakku" (truck), and "basu" (bus) are typical examples.

Firearms

The Japanese first acquired firearms from the Portuguese in the fifteenth century. Then, bringing to bear the iron production and forging techniques which had for many years been passed on for use in sword-making, they were quickly able to produce firearms on their own.

Japanese Computers

When computers first came onto the scene after World War II, it was widely assumed, both in the United States and in Japan, that since they were operated in English, they would never come into widespread use in Japan. Nevertheless, the Japanese then set to, and brilliantly succeeded in, the fiercely difficult task of creating computers operable directly in the Japanese language.

Westernized Inns and Japanized Hotels

As any visitor soon discovers, Japan is a place where Japanese-style inns which have been Westernized coexist with Western-style hotels which have been Japanized. At a Japanese-style inn, one finds units which are comprised of Japanese rooms and a corridor with a garden view, and which offer traditional maid services such as clothing, food, and bedding preparations. For those who so desire, however, there are also rooms with Western furniture and other such amenities. Conversely, at Western-style hotels, in addition to normal Western rooms, there are Japanese rooms as well as large public baths like those found at Japanese hot springs. And regardless of the type of room selected, customers are also given a choice of either Japanese- or Western-style service.

The Japanese are also particularly enthusiastic about creating or re-creating things which are convenient or practical. Consider, for example, the following.

From Industrial Arts to Fuzzy Logic

The modern industry of Japan started with the manufacturing of such materials as wax, lacquer, paper, kerosene, and silk prior to the production of mass consumer products like tiles, cloth, lacquerware, pottery, and textiles. Even in recent years electronics manufacturers like Matsushita Electric have been enthusiastic about bestowing higher levels of functionality to a variety of appliances including washing machines, refrigerators, air conditioners, and razors. Minute improvements of this type, and the resultant production of the so-called "fuzzy" products, are of timeless importance (see Photo 4.3).

Doubtless, Japanese companies have enormous faith in the value of innovation and the production of new and improved products. In their minds, any change should presumably bring about progress and assure better chances for success.

Production of New Products and Equipment

Sony's development of transistors and Honda's development of the CVCC original engine are well known the world over. According to Masaru Ibuka, Sony Honorary Chairman, he and Soichiro Honda, late founder of Honda, had one thing in common. "We, both of us, always aspired to pull from around us the raw materials for ideas and flashes of ingenuity," he said. "The truth of the matter is, we were both novices in engineering."[5]

One of the reasons for the success of Yoshida Industries, a fasteners manufacturer, is its policy of in-house design, construction, and improvement of all its manufacturing equipment. By putting to use such customer-developed equipment in all of its domestic and overseas factories, the company has been able to supply inexpensive, high-quality fasteners at high speeds, enabling it to gain the acceptance of overseas customers.

Searching for New Businesses

Partly due to the competitive climate, Japanese companies are as zealous about finding new businesses as they are about developing new products. Most companies–particularly the large ones–now have "new business development" divisions and make every effort to develop new businesses, as well as keeping a close eye on the movements of other companies in the same industry. When textile manufacturer Toray had only 750 million yen in capital, the company paid the huge sum of one billion yen to DuPont to acquire nylon manufacturing technology. This sort of development has been observed quite frequently thereafter as well. The most frightening thing to a Japanese manager is the prospect–or the impression people around them may have–of their company products and or business falling behind the times or becoming obsolete. Out of fear that this nightmare might become a reality, many Japanese managers are constantly on the alert to look for ideas or propositions that may contribute to the exploration of new or improved businesses for their companies.

The Distribution Revolution

Right after World War II, Shiseido cosmetics embarked on a reorganization of its distribution systems. Instead of distributing its

PHOTO 4.3. Electric/electronic goods manufacturers are competing to market one "fuzzy" product after another. *(Courtesy of Japan Management Association)*

products through traditional wholesale channels, the company organized them into a chain of 20,000 or so retail stores called, "Hanatsubaki-kai" (literally "Camelia Club"). This change was dramatic in that it was carried out in the tradition-bound distribution world, so dramatic that it was labeled the "distribution revolution." Ever since, Shiseido has been enjoying a leading position in Japan's cosmetic industry. This success is known to be the result of the company's farsightedness in reorganizing distributors and, through them, millions of cosmetics consumers across the country.

Kaizen

One facet of the Japanese sense of innovation is their methods and processes involved in organizing work. For instance, production engineers adopt numerical control devices, flexible manufacturing methods, and the like, in order to achieve cost reduction, quality improvement, and increased productivity.

On the production floor as well, just about everyone is a believer in, and practitioner of, method improvement, or kaizen. They are confident that wherever there is a method, there is a better method. Kaizen has become a watchword for the Japanese worker, and is itself a never-ending process.

According to Masaaki Imai, author of *Kaizen,* the faith in kaizen in Japan contrasts sharply with the mentality toward so-called innovation in the United States and Europe. "Innovation is dramatic, a real attention-getter. Kaizen, on the other hand, is often undramatic and subtle, and its results are seldom visible. While kaizen is a continuous process, innovation is generally a one-shot phenomenon."[6]

The results achieved by this sort of kaizen are by no means insignificant. Imai explains further. "At one major Japanese electronics company, the semiconductor laser developed for use in compact-disc players cost 500,000 yen in 1978. In 1980, it was down to 50,000 yen, and by the fall of 1981, it had been reduced to 10,000 yen. In 1982, when the first compact-disc players were put on the market, the semiconductor laser cost only 5,000 yen. As of 1984, it was down to the 2,000-to-3000 yen level."[5]

Small Group Activity

As discussed previously (see Chapter 1), since the 1960s, there has been a phenomenal development in Japan of the so-called "small-group" and corresponding "small-group activities." The number of individual small groups in companies has increased and the scope of activities performed by such groups has expanded. Variously called Quality Control Circle (QC), or Zero Defect Group (ZD), depending on the cause of its formation, the small group usually aims at two things–worker motivation and concrete results in terms of ideas and their implementation. Workers are motivated by having the opportunity to participate in decisions concerning increased productivity, quality, and safety, and improving company policy on the environment and their own working conditions. Employees usually see this involvement in management decision making as opportunity to learn about the company, improve their management skills, and, if fortune smiles on them, to gain recognition from upper management, which may lead to a promotion. The results of worker participation in small groups are varied, although the number of suggestions generated by individual workers–up to thousands of suggestions from one worker a year–can be dramatic.

As a concrete example of the types of issues being tackled by these small groups, Imai describes some of the reports presented by Quality Control Circles in November 1980.

> Most reports were related to production. For example, a leader from Kobayashi Kose spoke on how a QC circle dealt with the task of removing pits on the surface of lipstick. But there were also reports involving improvements in office work. For instance, Sanwa Bank, one of Japan's largest banks, has 2,400 QC circles involving 13,000 employees. Since the circles were started in 1977, they have dealt with 10,000 subjects. Being in banking, they defined quality as the level of service and the degree of customer satisfaction, and based on this definition, they strove to improve the quality of their office work.

> The subjects they are working on at Sanwa Bank included: how to reduce erroneous listings, how to route mail more efficiently, how to remember customers' names, how to save energy, how to save stationery, how to reduce overtime work, how to increase the frequency of customer visits, how to gain new accounts, and how to improve employees' familiarity with the many services the bank provides. All these subjects were dealt with by the bank's ordinary employees, such as tellers and clerks.

> The circle leader from the Kanzanji Royal Hotel, a typical hot-springs inn, explained how the hotel's QC circle approached the problem of serving shrimp tempura hot to 500 guests. The QC circle was so successful that hot shrimp tempura has become one of the hotel's main attractions. (Since food has to be prepared hours ahead of time for big groups, it is common for the major resort hotels to serve it cold.)

> Sachiko Kamata of Bridgestone Tire reported on how she had formed a "Queen Bee Circle" with four other draftswomen (the youngest one 19 years old) in the engineering department to improve the drafting procedures for tire-making jigs and tools. Holding two-hour meetings every week to obtain and

analyze the relevant information, they found that there was much redundancy in their drafting work and that the problem could be solved by resorting to a special application of photo-copying machines. "As a result of the new procedure," she said, "we have been able to reduce drafting time by 60 percent. Whereas we used to have an average of two hours of overtime every day, we have been able to eliminate overtime work."[8]

RELATED TRENDS AND PERSPECTIVES

There are no signs that the curiosity of the Japanese will ever change, particularly with respect to things that are novel or come from abroad. They will most likely continue to keep their information antennas fully extended as they reach for new knowledge. The circulation of daily newspapers in Japan exceeds 70 million copies per year, with 500-some-odd newspaper subscribers for every 1,000 people in the country. This figure ranks high among the countries of the world.

Businesspeople as well, through foreign study tours and other means, are likely to continue to aggressively pursue the new and improved. They can also be expected to continue to devote their energy toward adopting new technologies and new systems. And their faith in kaizen and efforts at innovation will certainly continue with no end in sight. The Japanese, while placing significant emphasis on tradition, will not hesitate to shift their thoughts and actions toward the quest for practicality. Japanese do not consider these concepts to be mutually exclusive at all.

As for the question of whether or not Japan's various efforts at innovation can be called imitation, opinions in Japan are still divided. Some, for example, take the view that the Japanese way is to use something which already exists as a starting point, and then to proceed to create something which is uniquely theirs—that this is a process of "distillation" or "Japanization."

For example, Tetsuzo Tanikawa, author of *The Japanese Mind*, states that "Although Japan borrowed much from Indian and Chinese cultures in terms of architecture, sculpture, painting, scholarship and religion, in each case Japan reworked these borrowings into its own unique style–in a process that required an independent spirit of creativity."[9]

Ken-ichi Fukui, Professor Emeritus of Kyoto University, points to how Japan's adoption of Western science and technology in the early Meiji Period enabled it to become one of the leading industrial powers in the world in a remarkably brief time. "There are those," he states, "who would claim that Japan's talent is nothing more than the simple ability to imitate. However, I do not feel that this is the whole story. My reason for feeling this way is that in order to keep ahead in the advanced fields of science and technology, constant improvement and advancement must be carried out, and in order to accomplish this objective, both a high technology standard and an enduring creative imagination are required. This would be quite impossible through mere imitation."

There are also businesspeople, among them Sony Chairman Akio Morita, who clearly affirm the creative tendencies of the Japanese. "For a long time, the Japanese have been branded as imitators rather than creators. But I think it would be downright foolish to say that what Japanese industry has accomplished in the past forty years has been anything but creative. The work being done in biotechnology, new materials such as ceramics and fibers, optoelectronics, and other fields all speak for themselves. And certainly our contributions in production technology and quality control have been creative."[10]

On the other hand, the opinion is often heard that Japanese companies show a relatively strong inclination toward applied technologies rather than basic technologies. As one professor stated, "The Japanese appear to be poor at basic research which demands time and persistence. Instead, they tend to put more effort into the development of practical technologies that are directly tied to actual products."

These trends, i.e., "Japanization" and the emphasis on applied technologies, are likely to continue in the future, and the viewpoints of the Japanese on the subject will remain diverse.

REFERENCE NOTES

1. Gregory Clark, 1977. *The Japanese Tribe: Origins of a Nation's Uniqueness* (The Japanese translation: *Nipponjin: Yumikusa no Gensen,* by Masumi Muramatsu). Tokyo: Simul Press.

2. Iwao Nakatani, 1989. *Will,* p. 34.

3. *JMA Management News*, May 10, 1991.

4. Akira Totoki, JMA chairman. Interview with author.

5. Masaru Ibuka, 1991. *Waga Tomo Honda Soichiro (My Friend, Soichiro Honda).* Tokyo: Goma Shobo.

6. Masaaki Imai, 1986. *Kaizen.* New York: Random House.

7. Ibid. p. 33.

8. Ibid. p. 99-100.

9. Tetsuzo Tankiawa, 1988. *Nipponjin no Kokoro (The Japanese Mine).* Tokyo: Kodansha.

10. Akio Morita with Mitsuko Shimomura and Edwin Rheingold, 1990. *Made in Japan.* Tokyo: Asahi Shimbunsha.

Chapter 5

Respect for Form and Hana Yori Dango

One cannot fight on an empty stomach.

Though he may have no food to eat, the samurai picks his teeth clean. (Even when a warrior has no food, he acts as though his stomach is full.)

RESPECT FOR FORM

The Japanese are trained from very early in their lives to act in accordance with established forms of behavior. From the time they enter kindergarten, they all become accustomed to having the same uniforms, hats, and carrying bags, and are taught to always address their parents, elders, and teachers with respect. School rules typically regulate clothing and hair length, as well as what students are allowed to do outside of school and even what coffee shops they are allowed to enter.

Further, upon becoming adults, the Japanese are expected to observe even more rituals and customs. Included among these are rules of etiquette based on age and gender, such as the addressing of superiors by their last name followed by the suffix "san"; the use of a superior's first name after achieving a rapport, as is common in the United States, is simply unthinkable. When men and women take the same elevator, Japanese women will almost without exception stand behind the men and get out last.

Even when receiving a gift, a Japanese individual will commonly refrain from opening it in the presence of the giver, simply expressing his gratitude and taking the gift home. This is a custom which was established in order to avoid the potential embarrassment of one or both parties.

Upon visiting someone else's household as well, the Japanese are expected to do a number of things when invited to enter. For instance, after the visitor removes his or her shoes–which is required in just about every Japanese home–he or she then picks up the shoes and points them toward the door and places them as far in the corner as possible. It is, in addition, preferable for women to perform these acts on their knees.

Nowhere is the Japanese respect for ceremony more apparent than when getting married. This is even more so when importance is being placed on the relationship between the two families. As typical formalities before tying the knot, for example, an individual who will act as "matchmaker" is solicited, the marriage proposal is performed through this matchmaker, engagement gifts (money and valuables) are exchanged, the respective parents and other family members are introduced, a dinner bringing together the families is thrown, engagement rings are exchanged, and on and on. This applies primarily to traditional arranged marriages; however, even in the case of "love-based" marriages, despite the possible absence of some of these elements, the same basic conventions are observed.

Formalism sometimes manifests itself even in situations which are purely for entertainment. When the Japanese play recreational baseball, for example, they invariably change into uniforms, whereas in similar situations Americans typically just show up on the field in jeans and T-shirts. Likewise, whether it be dancing, skiing, or anything else, the Japanese usually insist on studying all aspects of the activity with a teacher or expert beforehand, while Westerners are more inclined to learn by doing.

Shizuoka University Professor Shuji Hayashi cites another enlightening example. In Japan, he explains, it is quite common for people to go on one-day excursions to collect chestnuts in the mountains or gather seashells at low tide. But because there are often not enough chestnuts or shells to go around, workers are often dispatched each morning to bolster supplies of these items for visitors to "find." These unknowing visitors then take great pleasure in gathering what they assume to be products of nature "in the wild."[1]

Businesspeople also observe and adapt to a variety of rituals, formalities, and ceremonies (see Photo 5.1). These range from first-time meetings to the presentation of souvenirs, from new employee gatherings to retirement parties. People equate these affairs with group order, with ease of teaching and learning, with efficiency, or simply with reverence for tradition.

First-Time Meetings

Upon meeting someone for the first time, a businessperson will first bow instead of shaking hands. Shortly thereafter, business cards are exchanged. The nature of the bow will vary from fairly shallow to extremely deep and respectful, depending on the rank and relevance of the other party, or on the relationship with the other party's company. As with people in business anywhere in the world, the exchange of business cards by relevant parties is pretty much automatic. However, when business cards are exchanged between Japanese, it is not only to find out the other person's name but also their rank, as this information is used to determine how to treat the other person. In this sense, the exchange of business cards can be said to fulfill a practical function above and beyond mere formality.

Titles

Businesspeople in Japan are similar to businesspeople in the West in that they are given titles based on their rank in the company, from the chairman and president on down. Compared with other countries, however, the extent to which these titles are emphasized by their colleagues, their families, and even society as a whole, is extremely high. Japanese say, "Names reveal substance." In addition to ability, a person's title represents standing, track record, and popularity within the company. It is also taken as a fair indicator by third parties who value trust. Titles are thus accorded a high degree of importance by a great many Japanese. Some of the most respected titles in Japanese society include high-level government officials, university professors, artists, prominent business executives, and other professionals.

PHOTO 5.1. Businesspeople also are image conscious and love ceremony. A tape-cutting ceremony is often an important part of the opening of a new event or a newly completed building/facility. *(Courtesy of Japan Management Association)*

Position titles most commonly used–and the most commonly adopted translations in English–are as shown in Table 5.1. Such titles for positions of responsibility are fairly uniform throughout Japan, so that relative ranking may be easily understood. In recent years, however, a number of variations have been added to these titles, most notably the tendency to attach prefixes like "fuku" (vice), "ji" (assistant), and "dairi" (deputy). Companies tend to give such titles–if only insignificant ones–in an effort to motivate their staff.

Clothing

Japanese factories make it a practice to provide work clothes, headgear, and safety boots to just about everyone, from factory manager to the janitor. Many offices provide uniforms primarily for

TABLE 5.1. Managerial Position Titles within Japanese Organizations

Kaicho	Chairman
Meiyo Kaicho	Honorary Chairman
Shacho	President
Fukushacho	Executive Vice President
(Seisan Tanto) Fukushacho	Vice President–Production
Senmu Torishimariyaku	Executive Managing Director
Jomu Torishimariyaku	Managing Director
Torishimariyaku	Director
Jigyo Honbucho	Director of . . . Division
Fuku Honbucho	Assistant Director of . . . Division
Bucho	Director of . . . Department (General Manager . . .)
Jicho	Assistant Director of . . . Department (Assistant General Manager . . .)
Kacho	Manager of . . . Section (Chief of . . . Section)
Kakaricho	Manager of . . . Branch (Chief of . . . Branch)
Soudanyaku	Counselor
Komon	Advisor
Kansayaku	Auditor
Jonin Kansayaku	Standing Auditor
Kojocho	Factory Manager
Shitencho	Manager of . . . Branch Office (Chief of . . . Branch Office)
Shocho	Manager of . . . Office) (Chief of . . . Office)
Kenkyushocho	Director of Research (Manager of . . . Research Institute)

women, and this practice is obligatory in places like banks. Men, on the other hand, are expected to wear conservative suits, ties, and shoes. These types of uniforms exist mainly for workplace safety and cleanliness, for maintaining order, and for sales reasons. In some cases they are mandated by the company, and in other cases are for personal welfare.

Japanese organizations are beset with a wide variety of systems which have been propagated through the years. This inculcates in each individual the notion that he or she must in life abide by such norms and systems. The following are some especially conspicuous examples.

New Employee Ceremony

The indoctrination of businesspeople working in an organization to the required rites, rituals, and ceremonies begins on day one of their employment. Most Japanese companies bring in new employees in April of every year, and in large companies which hire as many as 100, 200, or 500 people, they are brought together on a day in March or April for a new employee ceremony (see Photos 5.2 through 5.6). And like it or not, these new individuals are required to participate.

As a hypothetical example, suppose you have been hired by M Corporation, an engineering company in Nagoya. You are first invited to be at Harumi Wharf in Tokyo on March 31 at 2:00 p.m. At 2:00, you find yourself together with about 500 other new employees, and you get on board the Nipponmaru, a luxury liner which the company has specially chartered for this occasion. Also aboard the ship are about 80 of M Corporation's directors. Before long, the ship leaves the wharf and sets out seaward.

Training soon begins for all of you seabound rookies. After the training ends, a party gets underway. You sleep on board the ship that night. The next day, April 1, at 10:00 a.m., the ship returns to Harumi Wharf, and you are invited to yet another employee ceremony, this time on more solid ground. There, the employees first proceed with self-introductions. Next, though a rarity in Japan, the company president himself shakes hands with each new employee individually. After that, a number of welcoming events are put on,

PHOTO 5.2. Ceremony for newly-hired employees in a large company. Most Japanese organizations bring in the majority of new employees on April 1 of every year. *(Courtesy of Japan Management Association)*

such as a quiz game with extravagant prizes. An hour and a half later, the ceremony finally comes to an end.

For this single set of events, M Corporation might spend a phenomenal 150 million yen. Granted, though, this may have taken place during a worker shortage.[2]

New Employee Education

One company in Kyoto is famous for its "purification" training for new employees. In this case, "purification" implies washing the body in pure water and cleaning away impurities–in the chill of early April, the company actually makes its new recruits plunge into a nearby river in their underwear. "It is our hope," the compa-

PHOTO 5.3. All the newly hired employees are called on to assemble together on day one of their employment, to receive "'jirei" (official letter of employment) and hear words of greetings and encouragement from company management. (Photo courtesy of *Management 21, Japan Management Association Monthly Magazine.*)

ny explains, "that this will provide a chance to throw out cold logic and go a little crazy and see things in a new way."[3]

Greeting Technique Education

The importance of bowing to Japanese businesspeople has already been mentioned, but in Japan this concept is even applied with respect to the shoppers in department stores. This means that the salesmen and saleswomen at these stores receive education in the greeting of customers. Bowing, for example, has been formalized into three categories: trainees are instructed to use a 15-degree shallow bow for simple greetings, a 30-degree bow when giving thanks for making a purchase or visiting the store, and a 45-degree bow when for some reason an apology must be made.

The result? You, the customer, step into a department store as it

PHOTO 5.4. At the ceremony for the newly hired, the company president personally shakes hands with each new employee individually. (Photo courtesy of *Management 21, Japan Management Association Monthly Magazine*.)

opens at 10 o'clock. As you do, the store's uniform-clad salespeople are lined up on both sides of the entrance, bowing together and greeting you with a hearty "Welcome!" You also get this same reception from the store's salespeople when you get to the escalator, from the managers standing at various parts of the sales floor, and from the elevator girls as well. Every employee thus observes some fixed system for greeting the customers.

Morning Meetings

In many companies, either every morning or on Mondays at least, the employees in the same division or on the same floor gather for a pre-work meeting. At this meeting, the activities planned for that day or that week are presented, any notable issues from the head of the workplace are discussed, and other relevant information is covered. In addition, either before or after these tasks, in some

PHOTOS 5.5A and 5.5B. After the ceremony, a quiz game with extravagant prizes is held as a part of the welcoming event. (Photo courtesy of *Management 21, Japan Management Association Monthly Magazine.*)

PHOTO 5.6. All the newly hired are invited to be at Harumi Wharf of Tokyo, to be aboard a luxury liner specially chartered by the company for ceremony and orientation. And yet another ceremony awaits them when the ship returns from an overnight cruise off Tokyo. (Photo courtesy of *Management 21, Japan Management Association Monthly Magazine.*)

companies the workers will sing the company song together, and possibly participate in some group calisthenics. When all of this is finished, business finally commences. Companies which value these customary morning meetings include some Japanese subsidiaries abroad as well. Honda of America Manufacturing in Ohio is one such example. Reportedly, the entire staff of this factory gets together every morning at 7 o'clock and discusses notable problems and concerns.

Seating Arrangements

Although not quite as strict as the department store bowing techniques, organization members are taught and expected to observe what are more or less seniority-based seating arrangements. These seating arrangements, which basically express reverence for elders, superiors, and customers, are considered important not only at formal meetings but also when eating or participating in informal gatherings. In general, in an organization's reception room, the couch is for customers, while the seats at the far end of the room are endowed with the highest degree of importance.

Formalization of Group Decisions

Of the various decisions made within Japanese organizations, a good number are fairly formality based, both in terms of the process of decision making itself and its announcement.

Ringi is basically a system of circulating simple proposals among, and obtaining concurrence from, the relevant members of an organization, and thus it functions mostly as a formality. The matters which are decided via ringi are more or less organization's routine, such as a business trip by a section manager, proposed revision of part of company rules or regulations, purchase of an inexpensive supply item, and the like.

Large Meetings

Meetings in Japanese organizations are often held as a matter of formality and do not readily lend themselves to group decision making because of the number of participants in attendance. Some of the internal officers' meetings in large companies and many board of directors' meetings are cases in point. Often such meetings are attended by 30 to 40 members and as such tend to become "rituals" in that most decisions are made perfunctorily on the basis of one-way presentations rather than in-depth discussions.

Middle-Up Decisions

In Japanese organizations, middle managers often make decisions for the sake of top management. If in agreement, the latter then formalize them either in their own names or as an "organization decision." This middle-up decision making, formality oriented as it may be, serves practical purposes as well. It helps motivate and develop middle managers and contributes to smooth implementation of the decisions at a later stage, as Mitsubishi Space Software's Yamaki pointed out (see Chapter 1, page 25).

Intra-Company Movements

Just as community groups stage "Red Feather" movements and various other campaigns, Japanese companies or factories also advocate various internal "movements" or "campaigns" of their own and solicit employee involvement. For example, there might be a "Safety Week" during which the importance of workplace safety is stressed, or a "Quality Month" during which efforts toward the improvement of product quality are encouraged.

The employees, on their part, see this both as a formality and as another challenge for internal competition, and, during the time frames of specific movements, most concentrate on putting in extra effort to ensure that the sought-after goals are achieved.

As in the case of Hitachi's "MI Movement" (MI being an acronym for Management Innovation), some of these drives are directed toward lofty objectives that span several years.

Among the more popular movements in recent years are the "5S movement,"[4] already discussed in Chapter 3, and the "Zero overtime day movement." Reflected in the latter campaign is the objective in the minds of both management and employees to materialize a shorter work hour habit by designating one particular day every week (usually Wednesday) as a day of no overtime work. Just how long this popular movement will last is yet to be seen.

HANA YORI DANGO

Hana yori dango literally means "dumplings before flowers" or "material rewards before recognition." Self-preservation is nature's first law. In certain ways the Japanese, with sayings like "Though he may have no food to eat, the samurai picks his teeth clean," show a respect for form, ritual, and tradition. On the other hand, with sayings like "One cannot fight on an empty stomach," Japanese also value obtaining the things that will satisfy their hunger, along with necessities. Their ancestors were an extremely utilitarian bunch, greedily grabbing up anything that might be useful in their lives, whether it be food, clothing, medicine, or language.

With the ultimate goal of achieving high status, high salaries, and other trappings which success entails, Japanese schoolchildren work extremely hard not only in school, but in many cases in so-called juku (preparatory schools) as well. At home it is not unusual for school children to stay up late studying every night. The majority of parents also believe that the future happiness of their children will be guaranteed if they are admitted to a top university and then employed by a name company.

Upon actually graduating from college, young Japanese proceed to demonstrate their material standards as they embark on the employment selection process. As the basis for their decision, those who are concerned about making a steady living will exhibit a preference for companies which have high salaries, companies which are stable, and companies which are growing. For those whose primary consideration is not financial, the nature of the work itself and the opportunities to learn will be weighed heavily. Many people in recent years have tended to fall into the latter category.

Previously mentioned Professor Shuji Hayashi points out that the Japanese exhibit a preference for the material over the intangible, and that this tendency is more apparent in young people. This observation is based on a comparison of people from Japan, Korea, and Taiwan which Hayashi conducted from 1979 to 1981. In the comparison, the percentage of people who stated that they valued "recognition over material rewards" were 71.7 percent in Korea, 56.0 percent in Taiwan, and 46.1 percent in Japan.

The question asked in the study was as follows: "Some people think that if a person makes a contribution to society, some kind of formal recognition–an honorary degree or a medal, for example–is sufficient, and a material reward is secondary. Other people believe that monetary compensation is preferable, with intangible recognition secondary. With which point of view do you sympathize?"[5]

The Japanese do exhibit an eclectic attitude even toward religion. Many observe Shinto ceremonies, and most weddings are in fact held in the Shinto style. On the other hand, almost all funerals are conducted as Buddhist rites. Meanwhile, Shinto itself has come to be seen as a tool for petitioning for worldly rewards such as abundant harvests and household safety, along with such things as success in business, success in exams, and painless childbirth.

The Shinto religion exhorts devotion to deities of natural forces and veneration of the Emperor as a descendant of the Sun goddess. In a 1983 NHK study, the Japanese were found to be 3.4 percent Shinto, 27.0 percent Buddhist, 1.5 percent Christian, and 65.2 percent nonreligious.

As shown in the examples below, many Japanese demonstrate various forms of pragmatism after becoming businesspersons as well.

Emphasis on Advancement

While taking great pains to work for the good of the team and to maintain the harmony of the group, many Japanese businesspersons also engage in subtle competition in which they attempt to outdo their peers if even just a little. In so doing they expect to reach for personal compensation: high praise and the salary increases, promotions, and other rewards that it brings. There are some who show interest only in those activities which will have a direct bearing on promotion in rank in the company, such as participating in golf or mahjong in order to ingratiate their superiors. Obviously, the name of the game is recognition, advancement, and remuneration.

Company Loyalty

The question is frequently raised, both among Japanese and non-Japanese, as to whether Japanese employees are truly as loyal to their companies as they are said to be. Those who express such doubts contend that employees do not really pledge their undying loyalty to their companies, but rather merely give this impression for economic reasons. Inarguably, in most cases money is indeed the greatest "dumpling" of all.

Overtime

Similarly, the question is often raised as to why Japanese workers work so hard and long compared with their counterparts in other countries. The 1989 survey by the Office of the Prime Minister in Japan partly answers this question. It revealed that whereas half of the Japanese workers are desirous of getting more free time even if it means no increase in salary, one-fifth still prioritize income over time. They have a saying, "For some, necessity is a hard master."

Lifetime Employment

This traditional practice has been in existence for over one hundred years in Japan, since the early industrial period, and for many practical reasons, both for management and labor. For management–especially in big companies–it has been a sure way of attracting and retaining a sufficient number of hands especially when manpower was in short supply. At the same time, the system has nicely fit with the practical sensibilities of workers, as it represented for workers steady employment, and hence steady income, educational opportunities often at company expense, and, for some, even the chance of finding a marriage partner, among other privileges.

Under this system, workers are often motivated by the notion that "The longer I stay with this company, the greater the chances for me to enjoy these special benefits, and the harder I work, the greater my contribution will be to the success of the organization, which in turn will be reflected in my share of the fruits of my labor, monetary and otherwise."

The pursuit of "dumplings" is of course demonstrated by groups as well, as shown in the examples below.

Contracts

When drawing up a contract or agreement between two organizations, Japanese tend to consider it more or less a target for future efforts, not a final, binding agreement. They take the view that assumptions and contexts are bound to change with the passage of time, and that it will be more practical to assume that when the situation has changed, both sides should meet again to discuss and re-evaluate the situation. Comments Robert March, an international negotiation consultant: ". . . most Japanese assume that right and duties under the contract, even when written down, are provisional or tentative rather than absolute. Instead of trying to spell out all possible contingencies and provisions for enforcement in inflexible terms, the Japanese prefer to handle problems as they arise, often recognizing the doctrine of 'changed circumstances.' "

In most Japanese contracts or agreements, in fact, issues are described based on the assumptions and contexts which exist at a particular point in time. However, the actual content tends to be vague and often has little function beyond mere formality. There is one thing that Japanese will do, and that is to include in the contract or agreement a condition that, in effect, "If conditions have changed and any doubts have arisen with respect to the original agreement, they will be resolved through deliberations between the two parties." This leaves room for negotiation in light of changes in the circumstances. Perhaps most important is the feeling that the spirit behind the interaction is more important than exact legal wording.

Employment Conventions

In 1972, a document titled "Employment Conventions" was adopted by the Central Employment Measures Council, a group that represents universities, industrial firms, and the government (Ministry of Labor). The idea was to restrict company recruiting of university students before certain dates of the year (e.g., the summer of senior year) so that students may be encouraged to concentrate on their studies and companies may be advised to avoid too early a recruitment effort. For example, for the fiscal year 1989, August 20 was set as the date companies could start scheduling visits or "company orientation meetings" for interested students. October 1 was the date when employers could start telling individual applicants if they would accept them for employment in April of 1990.

In reality, however, some self-centered companies do start picking and choosing good students before the "season" opens, putting their "honest" competitors at a disadvantage. As a result, "Employment Conventions" have been revised almost every year to combat this unfair practice, but some companies continue to neglect the rules. Therefore, it is safe to say that these rules are high-profile, but essentially meaningless, documents.

RELATED TRENDS AND PERSPECTIVES

From greetings to meetings, the formalism valued by the Japanese is for the most part rooted in tradition. For this reason, most people in Japan conform with these rites and rituals happily and without resistance. When attempting to get something done, people simply select the established form which is appropriate for the situation; this procedure makes it easy to gain the approval of most people. It is thus likely that respect for form will continue to be an important part of the Japanese value system for a long time to come.

Nonetheless, these formalties can be divided into two categories, those which ultimately prove impractical and are eventually discarded, and those which linger in the hearts and minds of the employees and become permanent guidelines for behavior. Predictably, rules which prove necessary and beneficial to workers such as "Even if it isn't necessary for your job, you should always put on your helmet when you enter the factory," or requirements for letters of recommendation and introduction, tend to last over the long run.

By contrast, those that have no real meaning and are only shallowly useful tend to be weeded out in short order. The ringi system for consensus building is one such example. Further, despite strong image-conscious tendencies, the tape-cutting parties found in certain ceremonies are likely to disappear or at least diminish in scale. The long string of congratulatory addresses made by numerous guests at parties and other events will also lose popularity.

Somewhere between the practical and the purely formal is the Japanese custom of the annual gifts known as the "chugen" and "seibo." Whereas there was at one time a call to abolish these empty formalities, they have nevertheless managed to survive and are likely to continue into the future. In passing, when a Tokyo department store tried to experiment by offering customers a choice of plain, inexpensive paper for the traditional Japanese giftwrap, only a scant 2.7 percent of customers chose the simple style. This is yet another example of Japanese adherence to tradition.

Another enduring Japanese tendency is to polarize form and content. For example, the process by which something is done is often more highly valued than the result. In Sumo wrestling, rating of the wrestlers is determined not only by their record of wins and losses, but also by how their matches were won and lost. In union negotiations, the "good faith" shown by management is often the deciding factor in hammering out agreements. In organizations, the extent of a team member's effort and competitive spirit is in many cases considered as important as, or even more important than, the results achieved. (In fact, this is one of the reasons why workers work overtime and give up weekends–ignoring the fact that this boosts the number of work hours they put in each year–to demonstrate their tenacity.)

As author and Japanophile Boye De Mente has stated, "Westerners are fond of saying 'I don't care how you do it. Just get it done.' The Japanese retort would be to say 'Don't do it unless you do it the right way.' "[6]

Another aspect of formality worship is the emphasis on uniformity exhibited among the Japanese. For instance, rather than following their own ideas, Japanese people tend to conform with the styles of behavior of those around them. If they see others using a "Walkman," they will also use one. If they hear that others are shampooing in the morning, they will do so as well.

A similar phenomenon is present in an organizational context as well. Companies more or less behave in step with the actions of other companies, based on what could be called a "follow the leader" mentality. The following are a few examples of this point.

Shortening of Work Hours

Several years ago, the Japanese government and companies launched a drive to reduce the annual work hours of employees. In the private sector, Matsushita Electric announced its plan to bring the annual work hours down to the level of 1,800 hours by 1993, and soon other companies followed suit with similar announcements. These developments took place not as the result of logical considerations and discussion relating to the subject, but were instead reported simply as another manifestation of "follow the leader" syndrome.

According to the Ministry of Labor, one reason given by companies as to why they did not adopt a five-day work week was that "other companies in our industry have not implemented such a policy." This was actually the second most frequently cited reason, with as many as 36 percent of companies claiming it, after the first, more business-related reason which had to do with the need to maintain good relationships with clients and affiliated companies, and others.

Philanthropy

Recently, a number of Japanese companies have adopted a variety of philanthropic activities. Yet, the consensus among critics is that this too is simply a result of a "follow the leader" syndrome, and currently many companies are abandoning these activities as financial pressure from the "bursting of Japan's economic bubble" mounts.

Capital Investment

Even in areas of capital investment involving huge amounts of money, some company executives center their decisions around the concept of "balance with one's surroundings," and, as a result, investments are often made which exceed the bounds of necessity. Comments Kikuo Suzumura, Senior Managing Director of Iseki & Co., Ltd., "The agricultural machinery industry was at one time quite enthusiastic about the use of robots, 'flexible manufacturing systems,' etc., and some companies did install such advanced systems–even to the extent of using it as a means of getting their night shift work done. The result? Over production and stacks of inventory, on the one hand, and reassignment of now superfluous workers as maintenance workers of the same new systems on the other–literally a waste of everything!"[7]

From overtime to "employment conventions," Japanese pragmatism is likely to continue for some time. People–particularly the young–will take a much more utilitarian attitude toward things which are seen as most urgent, necessary, or doable.

For example, participants in fields of study attempt to acquire from their teachers and textbooks the knowledge, methodologies, etc., which seem immediately applicable, while showing little interest in logic and principles. The "case study" method used at Harvard University has not been adopted in Japanese universities, nor in Japanese management education. Academics, students, and businesspeople in executive seminars show little interest in this approach because it is perceived as offering no immediate results or "correct answers," and therefore as impractical and lacking in benefits, or "dumplings."

Companies and the general public are similar in that they are both driven by immediately apparent benefits. People will generally not oppose the placing of vending machines on their streets regardless of the aesthetic damage they inflict on the neighborhood (see Photo 5.7). Many people also park their cars and bicycles in areas which they know to be illegal zones. Local business owners try very hard

PHOTO 5.7. People generally will not oppose the placing of vending machines on their streets; they tend to be satisfied with the convenience the machines provide even though they may inflict aesthetic damage on the neighborhood. *(Courtesy of Japan Management Association)*

to protect their own vested interests, fiercely opposing, for instance, the advancement of large-scale department stores.

Generally speaking, manufacturers see more value in so-called "seed-sowing development" which promises to deliver results in a relatively short time than in basic research that requires a great deal of time and money. In the case of distributors as well, many will handle anything and everything that money and space will allow as long as the products are good and the margins are favorable, and then turn around and simply suspend business with suppliers–regardless of their country of origin–if the product runs out or if the advertisements or margins are viewed as unfavorable.

From every standpoint, the emphasis on material rewards in Japan can be expected to continue unabated in the future. The Japanese consider making things practical and convenient to be for the most part synonymous with progress, and they are strongly driven by this attitude. They also exhibit a strong trial-and-error mentality, as represented by the popular phrase "Anyway, let's give it a try"– this can also be seen as one of the causes of their emphasis on the "dumpling" of material rewards.

REFERENCE NOTES

1. Shuji Hayashi, 1988. *Culture and Management in Japan*. Translation: Frank Baldwin. Tokyo:University of Tokyo Press.

2. *JMA Management,* 21, June 1991.

3. Makoto Sataka, 1991. *Tosei Kigyo Annai (Guide to Present-Day Industry)*. Tokyo: Shakai Shisosha.

4. Takashi Osada, 1991. *The 5S–Five Keys to a Total Quality Environment*. Tokyo: Asian Productivity Organization.

5. Shuji Hayashi, 1988. *Culture and Management in Japan*. Translation: Frank Baldwin. Tokyo: University of Tokyo Press.

6. *The Journal of the American Chamber of Commerce in Japan* , July 1991.

7. Kikuo Suzumura, 1984. "Mass Production is Out of Step with the Times." Japan Management Association Newsletter, No. 19.

Chapter 6

A Mind for Competition and Outlook on Rewards

God is always on the side of the big battalion.

When successful, the army is called the government forces; when unsuccessful, the opposition forces.

A MIND FOR COMPETITION

The Japanese are great believers in competition (see Photo 6.1). Whether in recreation or in study, they love to compete. In the old days Japanese workmen used to pit their skills against one another; that is how they felt their life worth. In the eyes of many Japanese, victory in competition is still a virtue worthy of great respect, while defeat is a disgrace which could mean banishment from one's group.

Competition among the Japanese is revealed symbolically through such terms as "examination war" and "examination hell." These phrases are a reflection of the way children compete fiercely in their studies to enter into preferred elementary schools, junior and senior high schools, universities, and, ultimately, name companies.

Historians describe Japan's competitive spirit as the result of living in a closely packed populace amid insufficient resources over the course of many centuries. Moving up in the world was also encouraged after the Meiji Restoration in 1868, and this can be viewed as having set the stage for the competitive spirit of the modern Japanese. The Japanese are, in addition, characterized by a propensity for "wholeheartedness," as well as a concern for

PHOTO 6.1. Japanese are great believers in competition. "When competitors spring up," says Masaru Ibuka, Sony's Honorary Chairman, "we also begin to spring into action." Result: Often a fierce competition among manufacturers producing similar products and entering similar marketplaces. *(Courtesy of Japan Management Association)*

"face." These attitudes comprise a strong impetus which drives their competitive spirit.

Businessmen are also unmistakably strong believers in, and practitioners of, competition. From barbers to *sushi* chefs, workmen pit their skills against their peers. Department store workers compete on the performance of individual stores. Factory workers compete from division to division based on, for example, the number of suggestions they submit.

Japanese tend to become more competitive when in groups than as individuals. Whether as members of a division, a section, or a project, they will compete at times with other groups in the same organization, and at other times with external rival groups. In either case, competitive goals are formulated and then systematically achieved. The following are examples.

Rivals Are Welcome

In general, Japanese companies welcome competitors to appear, and then welcome the subsequent competition with them. The belief is that this allows them to cultivate a fighting spirit and thus facilitates advancement. "Sony used to make sluggish progress in the five years following its release of the tape recorder, despite having the market all to themselves," recalls Masaru Ibuka, the company's Honorary Chairman. "But when competitors sprang up, we also began to spring into action."

However, because of this generous attitude toward competition in general, the Japanese often see many companies starting businesses in the same industry at the same time, often resulting in fierce competition. Several years ago, the Japanese market was suddenly full of different brands of rice cookers and driers for "futon" (bedding). In each case, some leading makers introduced their new products and a number of other companies immediately followed suit. The same was true with the so-called "dry beer," with practically all of the country's breweries following a leader with similar products and subsequently culminating in an intense sales war. For the most part, the Japanese do not share the American "not invented here" mentality. In other words, it is not where it is invented, it is what you do with it that counts.

Table 6.1, derived from the comparison made among American, European, and Asian (including Japanese) companies in terms of corporate objectives, shows that nearly 60 percent of all Japanese companies are placing priority on the maintenance and improvement of their market shares, second only to the increase in the new product ratio. Of particular interest here is the tendency of Japanese corporations to focus on such items as "increased ratio of new products" and "expansion and maintenance of market share," reflecting the orientation of Japanese executives toward business expansion over profitability.

Market Share Competition

Japanese business managers have a strong belief in gaining and then expanding a share in a market. For most companies, in fact, the number one priority is usually to increase the company share in all

TABLE 6.1. U.S. vs. Japanese Corporate Objectives

	U.S.	Japan
1. Maintain/improve ROI	83.2	35.1
2. Maintain/improve market share	65.3	59.9
3. Achieve capital gain for stockholders	46.5	3.4
4. Improve/strengthen international strategy	10.0	42.8
5. Streamline manufacturing/distribution	19.8	36.3
6. Improve product line	18.8	29.6
7. Increase new product ratio	22.8	65.1
8. Improve equity capital ratio	10.9	13.0
9. Improve public image of company	5.9	10.8
10. Improve treatment of employees	1.0	4.3

Source: Kigy Hakusho (White Paper on Corporations). 1986. Keizai Doyukai.

of its product lines. In their beliefs, the increased market share would promise, among other things, increased sales, which in turn would contribute to the economy of scale–mass production, lower-cost production, greater profitability, and more security in employment. With a strong paternalistic orientation for employee security and other worker benefits, Japanese employers are much more obsessed with market share–its relative size and long-term growth potential–than short-term profits or dividends.

Capital Investment

To deal with this market share competition, businesses are generally enthusiastic about investing in their plant and equipment. Statistics show that of all the investments made by Japanese businesses, approximately 30 percent are directed toward plants and equipment. Especially after the 1950s their business philosophy has been to invest heavily in new plants and equipment, to expand, modernize, and automate, and, at the same time, to work toward becoming increasingly cost-effective and achieve ever-higher standards of quality. This is an "investment now, profitability later" type of psyche, so to speak. With a career record spanning 30, 40, or even 50 years in the same industry, Japanese executives can and do assume risks with a high degree of confidence.

Zeal for New Products and Businesses

Japanese companies are at the same time extremely aggressive in developing new products and exploring new businesses. In the JMA annual fact-finding survey of management issues, "diversification and new business development" and "strengthening of product and technology development capabilities" almost always outweigh other management issues (see Table 6.2). In reality, many companies create special offices or have their senior managers regularly visit outside countries, in search of new ideas for products or business. Among the industry news in recent years have been Nippon Steel's entry in the leisure industry, Nissan Motors' development of the Be-1 model–an "ultra-modern" car–and NEC's release of the 98-series personal computers which would compete with its own 5200-series computer line. These examples all reflect the fervor with which Japanese companies approach the development of new products and businesses.

Excessive Competition

In the spirit of competition, Japanese businesspersons often utter business jargon "kato kyoso." This term refers to the tendency of manufacturers producing similar products and entering similar marketplaces to stage a fierce competition. Often, at a later date, they re-enter the same markets with better-quality or additional features, only to find other rival companies also coming up with similarly excellent products and going head-to-head on the market. Prices and after-sale services also make competition excessive, which causes some competitors to suffer additional burden and as a result forces them out of the market. For example, following World War II, the excessive competition among 100-odd camera parts manufacturers whittled the number down to the ten or so that exist today.

TABLE 6.2. Management Issues in Japanese Corporations

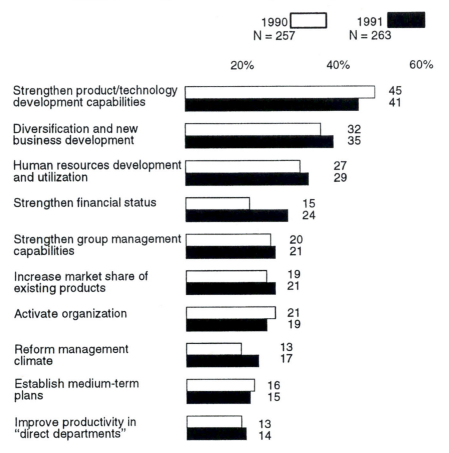

Source: Keiei Kadai (Fact-Finding Survey of Management Issues). 1991. Japan Management Association.

Competition by Improved Service Differentiation

Fierce competition is now being staged in the service arena as well. For one thing, manufacturers do everything possible to please end consumers, ranging from product line extension, size combination, and packaging to home delivery, payment terms, and servicing. Soon rivals follow suit, resulting in an intensive service competition among manufacturers. Then it is reflected in the competition on the retail level. This service competition is obvious if one watches small delivery trucks and bicycles racing around all day on city streets or if one listens to retail clerks calling wholesalers to have small shipments made to retailers three or four times each day. Apparently, the days are approaching when companies will be forced to compete by time-based differentiation rather than quality differentiation (see Photo 6.2).

Consumer Organizations

As discussed previously, Shiseido (cosmetics) took initiative over other companies in its industry in organizing a retail store and consumer organization called "Hanatsubaki-kai" with excellent results (see Chapter 4, page 75). Nowadays, Seibu and a number of other department stores are implementing similar competition strategies to establish a strong consumer network and expand sales.

Aversion to Mergers and Acquisitions

The Japanese market share strategy may be "all-powerful," as one puts it, but the idea of using tactics of mergers and acquisitions and other forms of corporate consolidation as a means of competition is not very popular, relatively speaking. One of the reasons is that the Japanese generally do not consider the merger and acquisition in a favorable light because of its implications in the change of management, the loss of jobs for some employees, and the loss of "face" for executives and shareholders, etc. When the government stepped into the auto industry after the war in an attempt to promote an integration of Japanese car manufacturers on a voluntary basis, the majority of companies–both large and small, and management and labor alike–resisted the proposition outright. In their minds, competition was more welcome than consolidation, even considering the resultant management stability in a surviving minority, as suggested by the government.

OUTLOOK ON REWARDS

The Japanese hold diverse opinions on money and profit. On one hand, they place a high value not on money, but on other things like

PHOTO 6.2. Japanese city streets are full of small delivery cars, trucks, and bicycles racing around all day trying to make small shipments to retailers or consumers–a new phenomenon of time-based differentiation rather than, or in addition to, quality differentiation. *(Courtesy of Japan Management Association)*

honor, trust, and personal worth. Some people even feel money is dirty, even contemptible, and to mention money or money making is simply not in good taste.

This view of placing money in a negative context is still alive in the hearts of modern Japanese. In his book, *Kankokujin ga Mita Nippon* (Japan as seen by Koreans), Lee Kun, an essayist, comments: "In Japanese society money is not the only emphasis. Rather, each individual seeks out his own personal source of value transcending value of a monetary kind."[1] It is said that the degree to which money is brought up as a topic of conversation between parents and children in Japan is extremely low compared with that in the United States. Tipping is another custom not found in Japan. It is somehow uncomfortable for both the giver and the receiver alike.

On the part of businesspeople as well, there is an inherent hesitancy to endow money with a role of primary importance. In fact, some are motivated to work for non-monetary reasons such as contributing to society. Even in business dealings, many Japanese are loath to discuss money matters in individual transactions, and prefer to do business on a long-term basis.

By the same token, until around the 1950s, Japanese companies did not place much importance on their sales departments or sales activities–another fact that testifies that commercial transactions were held in relatively low regard as was money making itself. When the American concept of aggressive salesmanship was introduced into Japan after the war, it did not actually meet with a very warm welcome at first. In those days, recommending some college graduate to become a company salesman could be taken as an insult–and a serious insult at that.

This trend has endured until very recently. At the time of the oil crisis of the 1970s, oil companies were accused of reaping excessive profits. Masaki Yashiro, the former president of ESSO Sekiyu, recalls, "There was a time, in fact, when companies were actually afraid of making a profit. Traditionally, profit-making has been spoken of negatively in Japan."

This view toward profit is, however, currently yielding to another, more realistic one in Japan–a perspective that was originally advocated by such leading scholars and businesspersons as Yukichi Fukuzawa (1835-1901) and Eiichi Shibusawa (1840-1931). These two men strove to demonstrate that profit is only a good thing if it is made in the process of striving for higher goals, such as benefitting society and the world at large.

Shibusawa asserted: "Profit should not be the primary motivation for business activities, but it will come in due course to those who take a long-range view of business planning, those who treat their employees justly and recognize them as the real strength of any enterprise, those who deal with their customers honestly, and those who tie the progress of their commercial endeavors to the progress of their country."[2] Many Japanese businesspeople currently share Shibusawa's viewpoint. Rather than being in business "only for the money," they believe that there should be some benefit to society along the way. Some examples follow.

"Don't Chase Quick Profits"

Sumitomo, one of Japan's typical financial and industrial con-glomerates (zaibatsu), made the slogan "Never chase quick profits" a company group's precept before World War II, and the group executives are known to have repeated this phrase literally all the time.

Yamato Transport's former president, Masao Ogura, affirms this by saying, "Customer trust comes first and foremost; profits are secondary." Ogura cites the following anecdote as an example:

> In 1986, the year in which the company started a ski transport service, the Nagaoka area was struck by a blizzard toward the end of December. As a result, we were unable to transport the skis to the resorts, but our customers were arriving there by train. We dealt with the situation by renting skis at the resorts, footing hotel bills, and dispatching additional employees from year's end until the third of January for support. This resulted in a loss to the company of 200 million yen, but I remember thinking at the time that money was not the problem. Rather, the problem was that if we failed (from a service standpoint) in our first year, we would end up failing permanently. Even now we feel that if we were to focus on the short term, our custom-er service would inevitably deteriorate.[3]

Social Contribution

Yukio Nishihata, founder of Nichii, one of Japan's four largest supermarket chains, on the occasion of establishing a new joint venture called Nichii Allied Chain, is said to have stated: "I have resolved to cast aside personal gains and to live for the public good, following the path devoted to serving my customers forever as a retailer."[4]

Society Friendly

In an interview with NHK (Japan's national broadcasting sta-tion), Tsuneya Nakamura, Vice-Chairman of Seiko-Epson, was quoted as saying that "Our company has a clear ideology . . . we are determined to continue to be a company which is friendly to the regional communities in which we live and the public at large. At the very least, we will not pursue profits via ways and means that are unfriendly to them. . . ."[5]

Cultivating Employees' Sense of Self-Worth

Many companies in Japan emphasize people over quick profits. Kotaro Higuchi, President of Asahi Beer, says, "It is not enough for a company to make a profit, it must provide a working environment in which employees can feel a sense of worth, and appreciate having an opportunity to work there."[6]

Focus on Long-Term Growth

As predominant corporate goals, many Japanese companies put growth before profits. The idea is that, although profits are important, too much emphasis on the bottom line can hinder corporate growth over the long haul, which in turn can have an adverse effect on profits. Thus it is fairly common for Japanese management to carry out massive investments in plant and equipment, technology development, human resources training, etc., so as to achieve market expansion and corporate growth over the long run–often at the sacrifice of short-term profits. This focus on the long-term growth on the part of Japanese companies is often contrasted with American corporations, many of which tend to have a relatively short-term orientation. Japanese find that the long-term approach typically produces better bottom-line results than on a quarterly basis.

Caring for Retailers

Yoshida Industries (fastener manufacturer) reportedly has been providing its retailers with inventory insurance on a consistent basis since World War II. What it does in fact amounts to this: When there is a 10 percent drop in the value of its products, Yoshida would pay its retailers to compensate for the loss in their inventory values. Says Tadao Yoshida, the company President, "If these other companies profit, our company prospers as well."[7]

Meanwhile, and unfortunately, there are still those who assign top priority to making money, who seek personal wealth by means of more or less unethical conduct or exclusionary practices, and who insist on protecting their vested interests at the expense of others. Despite this, the old Japanese adage that "Sufficient food and clothing facilitate courtesy and decorum," meaning that "Only when one's livelihood becomes stable can moral ethics prevail," is still very much alive.

RELATED TRENDS AND PERSPECTIVES

The Japanese believe in harmony, but at the same time believe in competition. Most Japanese hold that competition is synonymous with life worth, and this should continue.

Although competition that causes discord or disrupts harmony is frowned upon, if it serves some social advancement or peace, it receives massive support. What this means is that Japanese believe in both competition and cooperation, but in particular, they believe wholeheartedly that competition is the driving force behind social as well as economic growth.

The competitive sensibilities of the Japanese are quite strong on the company level. This is especially true in those industries where homogeneous companies are competing, as in the case of the automobile or camera industries. In other words, the companies in these industries are very much alike in their goals and internal sensibilities, which makes competition even more intense. This type of "industrial homogeneity" often lends itself to competition in the same basic conditions–product pricing, after-sale service, etc.

For some time now, doubts and criticisms have been raised regarding the competitive practice of Japanese companies, however. Many point out, for example, that the overwhelming emphasis on the market share as practiced in Japan is having an adverse effect in Japanese industry and in society at large, in that it tends to trigger "excessive competition," and as a consequence often forces unduly low levels of value added, or low margins, for manufacturers. This in turn tends to bring about lower employee salaries and shareholder dividends that will hardly compare with those in other advanced countries.

This debate over the pros and cons of the emphasis on increasing market share can be expected to continue for some time. While on one hand doubts are being voiced, there likewise seems to be some apprehension toward its revocation. According to a recent edition of the *The Wall Street Journal*, this issue is being re-evaluated even within famed market share advocate Konosuke Matsushita's company.

> . . . Matsushita was built on what the company called the "water tap" philosophy: Konosuke Matsushita, the company's late founder, constantly emphasized gaining market share, and preached the importance of turning out a steady flow of low-cost, high-quality goods. But company officials now concede that times are changing. Mass sales are out. Profit centers are in.[8]

The argument against the Japanese practice of low-level margins, salaries, and dividends was initially voiced by Sony Chairman Akio Morita in 1992, which was later quoted in a Tokyo magazine as follows:

> . . . On a comparative scale, Japanese companies pay their employees less for longer hours worked, take slimmer profit margins, and pay stockholders smaller dividends. . . . This competitive approach, fully accepted as necessary by society . . . does not translate well overseas.[9]

Aside from this debate on the market share practice and its limitations, critics are also taking issue with some Japanese manufacturers' efforts to make frequent model changes, add superfluous features to existing products, or use excessive packaging. Such practices, they claim, only reflect manufacturers attempts to add value or "keep up with the Joneses" and not the real consumer demand; they are a mere strategy for them to stay in business—a far cry from serving the public interest in the true sense of the term.

In effect, it is obvious that Japanese companies still have a number of issues to deal with as far as competitive practice is concerned. For example, how much should work hours be shortened, and under what conditions? How should the company's value added be distributed to labor, to shareholders, or to the community at large? How should manufacturers achieve symbiosis with subcontractors or suppliers? Also, some of the traditional practices, such as "dango," or collusion among competitors, will have to be addressed in an international context.

As far as profits or profit making are concerned, two lines of thought are likely to dominate the mainstream of the future. The first, which reflects the teachings of earlier business pioneers, will see it justifiable for companies to pursue profits in the course of conducting businesses for the sake of the society at large. Says Konosuke Matsushita (1989):

> ... I believe it is a corporation's duty to turn a profit and reinvest part of it in plant and equipment, as well as research and development. Without such investments, firms can neither come up with new and better products nor improve their services. . . . Profits are also necessary for companies to fulfill their social responsibilities in the form of taxes, dividends and philanthropic activities . . . . A private enterprise is a public entity, and profits make it possible for the enterprise to carry out its mission in society. . . .
>
> Thus I believe profit-making is a kind of virtue. Conversely, businesses that fail to make a profit are irresponsible, unworthy of existence. . . .[10]

A recent survey revealed that the Japanese have become considerably money conscious of late. In the past, there was a hesitancy among men and women alike to talk about money as it related to their living. Along with the desire for a more affluent lifestyle, however, a considerable number of young people in the working class now attach a greater importance to monetary wealth than ever before.

The second thought, which advocates the pursuit of profit in the spirit of free economy, admittedly is still prevalent and is likely to enjoy continued support among managers. The recent scandal in the Japanese securities industry, still fresh in the public's memory, serves to point out that this value orientation is still firmly rooted in Japanese society. Fortunately, however, this philosophy–and practice–when carried to an extreme, is met with criticism and is challenged by businesspeople themselves, as the following quotations from three business leaders amply demonstrate.

Masao Kamei, Chairman of Sumitomo Electric:

> . . . Even though financial engineering may work to a company's advantage, at the same time it inflicts a degree of damage on other companies . . . much like the players in a game of mahjong. . . . Business corporations should put an end to unsavory practices such as these. Inherently their function should be to produce tangible and intangible wealth, and their proper role should be to fulfill their social responsibility through provision of goods and services to society. . . .[11]

Sadaharu Sato, President of Sumitomo Marine Transport:

> . . . Profits are important for a private enterprise, but they should be realized as reimbursement for a devotion to consumer service and not pursued recklessly without regard to methods involved. . . .[12]

Konosuke Matsushita:

> [Profit-making is important], but this does not mean that profit-making should be the supreme objective of corporate activities; it should be considered as a means for realizing more important values, to achieve greater, more worthwhile objectives. In other words, profit-making must go hand in hand with business ethics. Unethical pursuit of profits cannot be justified . . . .[13]

REFERENCE NOTES

1. Lee Kun, 1984. *Kankokujin ga Mita Nippon (Japanese as Seen by Koreans).* Tokyo: Simul Press.

2. Jack Steward and Howard Van Zandt, 1985. *Japan: The Hungry Guest.* Tokyo: Lotus Press Ltd.

3. *JMA Newsletter*, January 1987. Japan Management Association.

4. Lee Kun, 1984. *Kankokujin ga Mita Nippon (Japan as Seen by Koreans).* Tokyo: Simul Press.

5. Katsuto Uchihashi, 1991. *Sonkei Okuatawazaru Kigyo (Companies Unworthy of Respect)*. Tokyo: Kobunsha.

6. Kotaro Higuchi. *JMA Management News,* May 1991, p. 7.

7. Lee Kun, 1984. Kankokujin ga Mita Nippon *(Japan as Seen by Koreans)*. Tokyo: Simul Press.

8. "Corporate Focus–Matsushita's Overhaul Effort Puts Emphasis on Profits." *The Wall Street Journal,* 1993.

9. "Morita Shock: New Paradigm Needed for Japanese Management," *Tokyo Business Today,* March 1992.

10. Konosuka Matsushita, 1989. *As I See It,* 5th Edition. Kyoto: PHP Institute, Inc.

11. *JMA Newsletter,* July, 1989. Japan Management Association.

12. Sadaharu Sato, 1992. *Gekidou ni Ikiru Keieioka Kanrisha (Executives and Managers Who Survive in Times of Turbulence)*. Fukuoka: Rikigaku Kenkyusho.

13. Konosuke Matsushita, 1989. *As I See It,* 5th Edition. Kyoto: PHP Institute, Inc.

Chapter 7

Silence as Eloquence

Kuchi wa Wazawai no Kado. (lit: Better the foot slip than the tongue.)–The mouth is a source of trouble.

Silence is golden.

The pheasant that keeps its mouth shut is least likely to get shot; silence seldom harms.

As a people, the Japanese are more reticent than Westerners. They make fewer statements, and explain considerably less, and generally speak less often. Japanese parents and schoolteachers teach children to refrain from talking too much. If a child is talkative or too glib they are scolded as being gabby, shameless, vulgar, and overall impolite. Adults who speak their minds freely also tend to be scorned; their vocalizing is taken as a manifestation of impudence and thus they become subject to negative social pressures to stop.[1] Criticism tends to be especially harsh when directed against young people, women, or new members of a group.

Similarly, the Japanese are particularly conscientious about manners of speech and politeness. As a matter of practice, honorific words, expressions, or euphemisms are used. It is considered most appropriate to use indirect, implicit expressions as much as possible, or to come up with serene comments without resorting to excessive feelings or emotions. Many would avoid using direct or explicit expressions as they can be taken to be arrogant or inconsiderate. Being talkative is not only likely to be offensive to others' ears but can be harmful if harmony is to be maintained. Above all, talking too much can be equated with lack of sincerity. Well-chosen moments of silence in conversation with a Japanese are a more powerful way of influence and bonding than a long, uninterrupted flow of cleverly chosen words. One would do well to learn this rhythm of silence and indirect speech if one wishes to convey a sense of personal integrity and encourage trust. One may conclude that such an attitude of the Japanese is a polar opposite of the American attitude expressed in sayings such as "Dumb folks get no land," or "The squeaky wheel gets the grease."

Most Japanese businesspeople share this value of "silence as eloquence." Within business organizations members try to avoid being labeled "talkative," as a "chatterbox" easily invites aversion. Those who try to promote themselves through self-publicity are least likely to be accepted when compared with self-effacing types. Robert T. Moran, author of *Getting Your Yen's Worth: How to Negotiate with Japan, Inc.,* observes that, "Americans associate silence in a negative context: anxiety, hostility or awkwardness, but in Japan it can mean respect for the person who has spoken, or consideration of an important point. Silences in Japan are moments to be shared, not empty spaces to be filled with words."[2]

Sen Nishiyama, essayist, has this story to tell: "An American company in Japan had a job opening for a bilingual secretary, and several applicants responded. Interviewing them were the company's general manager (American) and the human resource manager (Japanese), and they met with individual applicants in separate rooms. Later, the results of the interviews were brought together, which revealed that the American manager evaluated those who had kept their eyes on the interviewer's during the interview and who had been active in expressing themselves even to the extent of challenging interviewer's views, while the Japanese HR Manager preferred those who had kept looking downward during the meeting, who had talked softly and who would never mention a word of disagreement. The company eventually picked the one that the Japanese manager had recommended; after all, she was to work for a Japanese company. . . ."

A senior Japanese bank executive told me the following, which is often heard of Japanese managers in Japan: "In Japan," he says, "people generally do not like too clamorous a manager; instead, they are fond of caretaker managers–those who value human relations."

Certain value orientations of the Japanese are likely to be the cause or effect of their businesspeople being more or less tongue-tied, reticent, or nonexpressive. The following are examples of these values.

Respect for Group Discussion

When Japanese sit together to discuss as a group, individual members are supposed to refrain from taking too much time talking, but, instead, wait until the group as a whole has had a chance to discuss things formally. The group's orderly discussion, often initiated by leading members, takes precedence over individuals' free-wheeling voices.

Avoiding Confrontation Risks

At times, talkative individuals may be welcome, but pressures are such that even these people tend to become reticent to avoid having, or facing the possibility of having, conflicts of opinions or confrontations with other individuals.

Inexpressive Organizations

Not infrequently, some Japanese organizations fail to keep their managers sufficiently informed, placing them literally "in the upper gallery." For example, policy changes made at the top may be passed down to middle managers only in terms of "final decisions" or as "conclusions" and without any formal explanation. Middle managers therefore may have a hard time explaining such decisions or conclusions to succeeding levels of managers without any formal explanations to satisfy them. Few managers will dare to mention their own personal interpretations or opinions, because doing so might endanger their positions within their organizations.

Wait-and-See Attitude

Japanese negotiators are inclined to think that "laying the cards on the table" before the other side does will not be to their advantage. They therefore tend to remain silent and keep a "wait-and-see" attitude until the other side comes up with some propositions.

Senior Members First

Because Japanese live in a hierarchical society, they have been socialized to respect individuals of high social or organizational rank, including people with seniority or who are older. As a result, even in the business community Japanese are accustomed to try to be reserved and let other individuals of rank or seniority express themselves first. If they are quiet or short-winded, then younger people may fill the space with some words . . . but only to the extent of keeping discussions going without becoming too awkward or impolite.

Language Sensitivity

There are some Japanese who are overly sensitive to others' remarks or expressions. When it appears that some such individuals are around, many Japanese tend to become dumb or, if they talk at all, talk very slowly by being selective in the words or phrases to be mentioned. Some of the Japanese shareholders' meetings are held under such circumstances.

In his book, *American Way*, Gary Althen suggests that when people talk to each other they exhibit a communication style that is strongly influenced by their culture.[3] What about the Japanese—businesspeople, in particular? Let's look at some common characteristics of Japanese conversation.

Preferred Discussion Topics

Among the Japanese, the most common topic of small talk is the weather, followed by each other's and their family members' health, the speaker's current physical surroundings–the room, the building they are in, etc. Up to this point, Japanese are comparable with Americans. After the preliminaries, however, Japanese may be fond of talking of general business conditions and, in that connection, even enquiring about how well the other side is doing business-wise. Japanese tend to avoid talking about religion and other controversial topics, although one often overhears friends or colleagues discussing matters which may be considered "too personal" by American standards.

Favorite Forms of Interaction

Ritual interchanges such as "Kon-nichiwa" (Hello!) and "Odaijini" (Please take care!) are fairly common. Many greetings are meant to be concerned with form rather than with substance, and yet some Japanese may take them seriously and start talking about someone's illness or misfortunes. Women tend to disclose more about themselves to other women. There are some who "talk too much" or who "take long turns"; and when this happens, some people may freely and frequently interrupt the speaker, while others may just try to be patient and stay silent.

Depth of Involvement Sought

Japanese tend to look for close, interdependent relationships with others. People want relationships in which there are virtually no limits to what the friends will do for each other. For Japanese, "friends who live nearby are more important than relatives who live far off." Japanese expect that relationships, once established, whether personally or business-wise, will be maintained over a long haul.

Channels of Communication Preferred

Japanese businesspeople depend on both spoken and written words as much as Americans do, but, in their preference to be indirect and inoffensive, Japanese tend to resort to a number of channels, and thus take a longer time to convey the same message than Americans do. Reasons for this include a desire to convey respect for the listener; the need to win support or understanding; the preference on either side to talk things over informally or face to face; the necessity to arrive at agreements that may be mutually satisfactory in the long-term context, etc. Japanese do not prize verbal agility. Also, when Japanese talk, they listen to and respect the other speaker's silence.

Level of Meaning Emphasized

Educated businesspeople pay more attention to the factual than to the emotional content of messages, although there are still occasions when people become emotional or sentimental. During difficult times, for example, senior managers may resort to "emotional appeals" in their arguments. On the other hand, Japanese do not always like people who are "too cool" or "too logical"; they tend to become suspicious of a person who shows little emotion during conversation or in dealing with other people. As well, there are those managers who, instead of giving specific orders or directives to their subordinates, just offer them "hopes" or "expectations," leaving everything else to the subordinates' judgment or their suggestions.

Japanese place small importance not just on speaking, but on writing as well. In a business context, for example, they are generally much less accustomed to preparing notes or memos for future reference than, say, Americans. When writing something down on paper, many tend to just note main points or essentials of the matter under consideration rather than elaborating on details. The assumption here is that a brief gist should suffice at least for those who are knowledgeable about the matter and that if they have difficulty understanding it or making sense out of it at all, they should come and ask for the explanation on their own initiatives.

Many also claim that the more subjects are detailed in letters–be it company policies, rules or regulations, or plain agreements–the less flexibility there will be in carrying them into effect–often to the disadvantage of everyone concerned. Some examples may be helpful.

Company Precepts or Principles

Most Japanese companies have either precepts or principles, or both, but the majority are expressed in a simple set of phrases and often in short versions.[4] Matsushita's "seven spirits" are just one example of many similar statements popular in Japanese organizations, which presents a striking contrast to the long-winded, well-written creeds of American corporations such as IBM or Johnson and Johnson.

Seven Spirits of Matsushita:[5]

1. Spirit of service through industry
2. Spirit of fairness
3. Spirit of harmony and cooperation
4. Spirit of struggle for the sake of progress
5. Spirit of courtesy and humility
6. Spirit of adjustment and assimilation
7. Spirit of gratitude

Matsushita employees recite these "spirits," or the company's basic objectives, at their morning meetings every day.

Company Policies

Similarly, Japanese company policies are not always clearly stated, again forming a marked contrast to those of Western corporations. Policy statements, if available at all, tend to be spelled out in abstract terms, or otherwise ambiguously written, resulting in employees' often citing it as one of the most unsatisfactory management practices they observe in their organizations. Little wonder that non-Japanese managers working in Japanese-owned affiliates overseas are reportedly having frustrations over what they conceive as the lack of specific company guidance or direction.

Job Descriptions

Within Japanese organizations, an individual's role is not spelled out formally in a job description, and each worker is expected to learn it either from his or her supervisor verbally or from specific jobs given him or her in day-to-day work. On the part of managers, many are skeptical about the use of the job description in the first place. Comments one manager: "It looks as though the job description is helping build a castle around a worker and make each an independent 'castle lord.' Each 'lord' may feel happy about it, but there are bound to be a lot of dead angles, or vacuum areas between or among such castles, which will have to be filled." Says another: "One of the manager's responsibilities, I believe, is to develop people. I suspect the task will never be achieved by means of letters of a job description; it is more likely to be done by giving them work day after day."

Contracts

As discussed previously (Chapter 5: Respect for Form and Hana Yori Dango), most of the contracts used in Japan are brief and compact, with the document often pronouncing only important points of discussion or agreement. Japanese contracts hardly compare with their Western counterparts which tend to be all-inclusive in nature.

The Japanese, in the first place, generally reject the idea of making so thorough a contract. It is, after all, a document which needs to be reviewed and readjusted now and again when the situation has changed or if one side has broken it. For Japanese, spirit–or trust–is more important than wording. As Robert March, an international negotiation consultant, puts it: "The fundamental Japanese approach to contracts is to emphasize the relationship being created, instead of the document being drawn up."[6] For example, when publishing a book in Japan, this writer had the same experience that most other Japanese authors are known to have: I started writing a manuscript one day based on a promise I made to a publisher verbally. It was after the manuscript was completed and handed over to the publisher that I put my seal on the contract that was then sent to me for signature and return!

RELATED TRENDS AND PERSPECTIVES

The Japanese, although more expressive today than ever before, still talk much less on average compared with other peoples of the world. Many Japanese are generous about each others' silence or reticence. Few Japanese are ever skeptical about those who fail to respond quickly as being impolite or crafty. This receptivity to silence, or reticence, is a deep-seated cultural trait, and is therefore likely to continue for years.

In the business world, people by necessity are more talkative and expressive than average citizens. And, yet, since there still is a deeply felt belief in Japan that "silence is golden" or that "the mouth is a source of trouble," many conscientious businesspersons will be pressed to make the best judgment between when they like to be self-assertive and when self-effacing. Those who assert themselves too strongly without much regard to what others are thinking or interested in will still be frowned upon.

The above notwithstanding, the general consensus today is that as they become more and more involved in relations with the so-called "low-context culture" people in the future, the Japanese will have to learn to be more eloquent in their speech. Many businesspeople say they know this will be another great challenge—a challenge as great or even greater than speaking the English language.

The issue of improvement on the part of Japanese in international communication as perceived by most Japanese businesspeople today may be summarized as follows:

- The need to become more outspoken and expressive. Even managers or supervisors often express things in general terms, leaving it to the judgment of individual subordinates just how to interpret it. When dealing with non-Japanese, most need to be encouraged to avoid using ambiguous expressions and, instead, state their views as clearly and understandably as they can, since vague statements not only can invite misunderstandings but are also taken as an indication that the speaker cannot be trusted. Relying on contextual inference, "mind reading," and conjecture needs also to be avoided.
- The need to apply more theoretical or deductive reasoning. The tendency to underestimate the theoretical or abstract ideas has long been a weakness of the Japanese, but in the future it will become increasingly important for them to become more theoretical or deductive when explaining points of view in domestic as well as international situations.

- The need for most Japanese to have to listen to criticism from non-Japanese. Criticism must become a more acceptable method for communication and improvement, and not be equated with censure, slander, or as face losing as it has in the past among Japanese.
- The need to overthrow the popular notion that the Japanese language is by its nature poorly disposed toward logical explanation. Former United States Ambassador Reischauer discarded this view as "balderdash" and added that "there is nothing about the Japanese language which prevents concise, clear, and logical presentation, if that is what one wishes to make. The Japanese language itself is fully up to the demands of modern life."
- The need to overcome the linguistic handicap and become more articulate, at least to the extent where Japan may be able to express itself to hold its position in a global society. Although the number of Japanese capable of speaking English is on the increase, unfortunately the number who are able to engage in English conversation on an intellectual level remains extremely limited. The consensus has been evolving for quite some time that more positive steps should be taken to cultivate skilled foreign language speakers or communicators.

Lastly, a mention may be made of the practice of referring to "honne" and "tatemae" as modes of intention or sincerity in Japanese speech, as this traditional Japanese communication style is likely to persist. "Honne" generally refers to what the speaker is honestly thinking, and "tatemae" refers to polite "sweet talk" or saying what the speaker thinks the listener wants to hear in order to keep the exchange flowing without conflict of any kind. In their daily lives most Japanese will tell others what is really on their minds. In fact, "honne" is by far more prevalent; most people would prefer to talk "substance rather than form."

Yet there still is the persisting possibility that some individuals may feed you a certain "official line"–"tatemae"–in certain formal social situations which call for political diplomacy or public courtesy, such as in a store, a formal business meeting, or an international public statement.

In the context of the present-day business society, one is more likely to encounter what may later turn out to be a "tatemae" argument when talking with someone who represents a group of people or organization, i.e., a company or government official. When speaking on behalf of a group or organization, some individuals become concerned about what effect their voices may have internally (on group harmony, etc.) or externally (on public image, etc.) and, as a result, may prefer only to say nice things about the groups or organizations they represent–things which may not necessarily reflect the truth of the matter or the real feelings of the members involved. One has to decide for oneself whether a statement or announcement made by such a representative is "honne" or "tatemae."

REFERENCE NOTES

1. When traveling on public transportation such as the bullet train, few Japanese strike up a conversation with the person sitting next to them. Most people seem to feel more comfortable with the solitude of reading a book, magazine, or newspaper.

2. Robert T. Moran, 1985. *Getting Your Yen's Worth: How to Negotiate with Japan, Inc.*, p. 90.

3. Gary Althen, 1988. *American Ways.* Yarmouth, Maine: Intercultural Press, Inc.

4. According to a survey made by a Tokyo private publisher, among the most frequently used words or phrases in the text of company precepts or principles are: "sincerity," "kindness," "harmony," "effort," "challenge," "courage," "trust," "quality," "enthusiasm," and "for the sake of the public."

5. "Sunao," Harvard Business School Bulletin, p. 21.

6. Robert M. March, 1988. *The Japanese Negotiator.* Tokyo: Kodansha International, p. 111.

Chapter 8

Perception of Time

Toki wa Kane nari–Time is money.

Isogabe Maware–Make haste slowly.

Hayaoki wa Sanmon no Toku–Early birds get the worm.

Ishino Uenimo Sannen (lit.: Three years on the stone)–
Patience is a virtue.

The two famous warrior generals of the Sengoku period (fifteenth-sixteenth century), Oda Nobunaga and Tokugawa Ieyasu, are often compared due to their different personalities. The former is quoted as having said: "If the cuckoo doesn't sing, kill the damn thing," while the latter is quoted: "If the cuckoo doesn't sing, let's wait until it does."

As the apocrypha story reveals, there are some Japanese who are short tempered and others who are long on patience. This dual nature of the Japanese character continues even today. Naturally, in certain instances the same individual may manifest great forbearance, and others may exhibit a total lack of patience. Many Japanese tend to lose patience, for example, when waiting for an elevator, even for a few seconds. They also do a great deal more complaining than non-Japanese when obliged to wait their turn at a hotel or airport check-in counter.

Meanwhile, at international seminars or lectures, most Japanese will sit patiently waiting for a foreign speaker's words to be translated consecutively into Japanese. (Americans exhibit far less patience in this respect.)

Japanese parties or ceremonies often start with addresses by host and guest representatives, and while this is going on all the rest of the guests in attendance are supposed to, and actually do, stand patiently for half an hour or longer with a glass of beer in hand!

The Japanese perception of time has changed in the past years, and today many Japanese, including businesspersons, attach a great importance to time–perhaps as much as, if not more than, Americans do. "Time is money" is true with most Japanese. One manifestation of their time consciousness is in keeping appointments or punctuality. The following are examples.

"On Schedule"

In meetings or visits of either a private or a business nature, many Japanese set great store by keeping appointments or by starting meetings "on schedule." (This is a far cry from the old days when the Japanese used to be notorious for the tardiness or sloppiness of meetings, visits, etc.) Today, more than ever, one's attitude toward punctuality affects the degree of trust that forms the basis of human relations. A sales representative who is lax about keeping appointments is viewed as lacking in manners and as a result tends to lose the trust of those he or she is dealing with–and eventually the business itself.

On-Time Delivery

In business dealings between two firms the key to a successful relationship often depends solely on the punctuality of deliveries. For this reason, Toyota's suppliers, for example, make particularly strong efforts always to deliver parts and components "just in time."

Consumers are also fastidious about delivery. For example, when a customer orders a suit or a piece of furniture, delivery is generally promised quite quickly–in many cases within a week. And in most instances this demanding delivery schedule is kept. In Japan, retailers know that the Japanese consumer places high value on swift delivery of purchased goods.

Some Japanese are speed crazed, too. It is not uncommon, for example, to find people who finish breakfast or lunch in a matter of five to ten minutes. History has shown that each time the country suffered from natural disasters such as typhoons and earthquakes, Japanese worked hard together to recover from such calamities with remarkable speed. Some observers call this "Japanese typhoon mentality."

At the corporate level, too, Japanese on the whole make efforts to complete tasks swiftly, and work that demands fast attention is often done with good speed.

On the Job

Japanese manufacturers are at all times striving to reduce their production cycle time to be more competitive. The following table shown in an issue of *The New York Times* illustrates that Japanese car manufacturers are ahead of other car makers in terms of the number of hours they spend to build a car by as much as ten hours.

A comparison of the hours needed to build a car.[1]

Regional averages:

Japan–domestic	17
Japan–U.S.	22
U.S.–domestic	25
Europe	36

Product Development

Japanese companies are generally faster than firms in other countries in developing products also. For example, Japanese auto makers develop new models in about three years compared with five to eight years required by car manufacturers in the United States and Europe.

This is not to suggest, however, that Japanese are at all times speedy in everything they do. To the contrary. In fact, at times Japanese are known to go about their business at a snail's pace.

Time-Consuming Meetings and Decision Making

The Japanese often take much time to build consensus among individuals concerned. They hold meetings frequently, some of which are literally a drag. They put in a number of hours–sometimes days–to make decisions, too. These time-consuming meetings and decision-making processes are being criticized, but they are still being justified within Japanese corporate culture as they make it possible for any number of people to participate fully in the information-sharing and decision-making process, and they often yield remarkable results later in the implementation stage, among other reasons. It is a deeply ingrained, well-respected social process in Japan to build consensus and therefore widespread support for the new policy or other decisions made. "Make haste slowly," they will say.

Slow Response

Unfortunately, Japanese society, including that of business, has its share of laid-back people and organizations. For example, some Japanese have a chronic failure in responding quickly to queries and other correspondence received from others–especially from abroad. There are people who are reported to be utterly negligent of such response. Government offices and large hospitals are notorious for being bureaucratic, inefficient, and time consuming.

N.I.H. in New Business Development

Contrary to the speed with which Japanese companies develop new products, Japanese organizations tend to spend a great deal of time developing new businesses. Here, American firms far excel in the swiftness of setting up new businesses, leaving their Japanese counterparts way behind and thus making them follow the American lead in almost every area of business. Examples of such "not-invented-here" businesses include convenience stores, fast-food chains, express delivery services, and car rental services, just to name a few.

Meanwhile, the Japanese tend to consider things in a long-term frame of reference. When deciding to select a residence, they normally assume it will be a place of permanent living and a place for their children to go to school for years. In looking for a job, they will expect to find a workplace where they can work for keeps–lifelong if possible. For most, a friend, once made, is someone to maintain a relationship with for ten, twenty, or thirty years rather than temporary or short term.

In the business world, too, most Japanese practices are based on long-term rather than short-term assumptions.

Focus on Long-Term Growth

Most Japanese organizations operate on the basis of a five- to ten-year plan, with their profit projections and investment plans geared to the company's long-term growth objectives. Few business managers believe in the value of short-term business operation. Just as average citizens adopt long-term views toward their own health, family savings, or children's education, so company managers find it most beneficial to keep from becoming obsessed with short-term profit or competition consequences. Almost all the stakeholders–main banks, trading partners, suppliers, and shareholders, as well as employees, will support the company's long-range plans, but rarely the short-term interest.

Capital Investment

Many Japanese companies undertake capital investment with a longer-range view than might average American companies. During the 1950s and 1960s the majority of companies in Japan invested heavily in production facilities as their foremost means of increasing capacity initially and then of achieving factory modernization, automation, and labor-saving objectives afterward. The Japanese belief in the aggressive long-term capital investment has been described by some as Japan's "investment now, profitability later" management mentality.

Lifetime Employment

Japanese companies–especially large ones–are well known for hiring employees on a long-term basis, often lifelong. Employees, on their part, also typically perceive of their commitment to work for the same employer long term. Through this system, Japanese companies expect to gain benefits that are not available otherwise–lower employee turnover, highly motivated, loyal workers, greater yields from training and education, and more stable labor-management relations, etc.

Human Resource Systems, and Training and Development

As indicated above, Japanese companies' human resource systems and training and development programs are all based on the premise that employees will stay with the company for years. Often the employee's length of service outweighs his or her performance in the manager evaluation for promotion or compensation, and similarly in the company training and development programs. For example, it is not unusual for a manager to evaluate his or her people more on the basis of how well they have performed in developing their subordinates or in increasing the morale of their group members over the period of a year or two rather than on how well they have achieved financially or otherwise over the period of three or six months.

Business Relations

It is a common practice for both Japanese managers and companies to establish and maintain business relations on a long-term basis. For most Japanese businesspersons, the ideal is to develop business relations into long-lasting mutually beneficial ones, be it between a manufacturer and a trading firm, between a wholesaler and a retailer, or between two partners sharing ownership of a joint venture. The so-called "keiretsu" system is an example of companies seeking direct or indirect benefits as a result of business relations of a long-term nature.

Strange as it may seem, while Japanese are generally long-term oriented, they simultaneously tend to focus on the present instead of the future. For most of them, what is happening at the moment is often more important than what may happen in the future. Nature, for example, is something to respect or succumb to, rather than to conquer as many Americans may feel. Most Japanese are bound by the thought that all the resources on earth, including space, are limited, and therefore need to be controlled or regulated. These perceptions, deeply ingrained as they are, lead them to assume an existentialist view of life, or to become pragmatic as we have seen already in the discussion of Respect for Form and Hana Yori Dango, in Chapter 5.

Consider the following account recorded by Professor Hayashi of Shizuoka University. It involves an exchange that took place at a meeting between a Belgian management specialist and a Japanese manager. The Belgian had been invited to speak to a group of managers on the topic "How Do European and American Management Methods Differ?"

The Belgian focused on time orientation in different countries:

> U.S. managers are situated in and work in the present, [yet] in running a business they are always future-oriented. . . . European managers operate in the present, but they always have an eye on the past . . . Japanese managers are neither future-oriented . . . nor past-oriented. They seem to always focus on the here and now–on immediate issues–so they are present-oriented.

One of the Japanese participants, a company president, voiced disagreement.

> You say Japanese managers are present-oriented, but I doubt it. My work takes me frequently to the United States, and I meet with many managers and chief executive officers. My impression recently is that we are more committed to innovation than they are. Two examples are the use of electronics in the automobile industry and the introduction of robots into small and medium-sized and traditional industries.

The Belgian was not persuaded, however.

> Japanese government and industry do not do real long-range analysis and planning. In the Japanese mode of analysis, even when thinking ahead, there is a strong tendency to posit the future as an extension of the present. There are very few speculative leaps into the unknown, attempts to consider it without

being bound by current interests and commitments. [Therefore] Japanese managers are present-oriented.[2]

In short, it would seem that the Japanese are both long-term- and present-oriented. On the one hand, for example, there are many parents who are future-oriented in the sense that they put great energy into educating their children, while on the other hand, many of the same people are, at the same time, merely trying to keep up with everyday needs.

RELATED TRENDS AND PERSPECTIVES

Naturally, some individuals fail to see wisdom in the view that "time is money." It is not difficult, for example, to find people who call on someone in his or her office or home without making an appointment, for no other reason than because they are "in the neighborhood." Also, it is not unusual for Japanese office staff–even managers–to visit their colleagues' desks to exchange information or even to ask a favor of them, without prior notice of any kind whatsoever. Some executives even welcome such intruders who suddenly show up for information or guidance!

Prior to the opening of a meeting or negotiations, many Japanese businesspersons prefer engaging in some small talk. This does serve the purpose of "breaking the ice," on the one hand, but it tends to cost an unbearable amount of time, on the other.

Also, in spite of the fact that many workers on the production floor work hard and most efficiently, there are still many who are less conscious of time, and end up spending undue amounts of time getting a job done albeit with plenty of good reasons–in order to pursue perfection in what one does, to offer service to others as best one can, to establish someone else's needs, to maintain good relations with others, or for whatever other reasons. These people tend to be obsessed with performing such tasks perfectly, but unproductively, often at the sacrifice of their own and their company's time. They will ask, "What is wrong in my hanging in there?"

This propensity to underestimate the value of time in favor of some immediate results is likely to remain unchanged. The Japanese long-term orientation will continue. After all, the long-term perspective has served the Japanese well in past decades, and it is unlikely that Japanese managers will want to change a good thing in the near future. Japanese companies, for example, will continue to honor, and even foster, faith in long-term dealings, as in the case of "keiretsu" relations.

For some years, Japanese have been discussing the matter of their working hours from the point of view of reducing them to enable workers to enjoy more time to themselves. Statistics show that the average Japanese worker in the manufacturing industry works over 2,100 hours per year–some 200 hours more than their counterparts in the United States and 500 hours more than those in the former West Germany (see Figure 8.1).

The consensus now is in support of this view. The average working hours, they say, should be lessened to around 1,800 hours per year–a level comparable to other Western industrialized countries. It has been argued also that such a goal could be achieved by several

FIGURE 8.1. Annual Hours Worked by Manufacturing/Production Industry Workers–Estimates for 1990

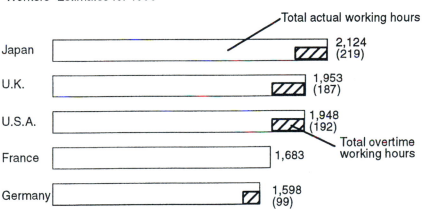

Note: Company scale: Those with 5 employees or more (Japan), all companies (U.S.A.), and those with 10 employees or more (others)

Includes regular part-time workers

Overtime working hours in the case of France is unknown

Source: Nippon, 1993 Business Facts & Figures, Japan External Trade Organization (JETRO)

means–less overtime hours, more strict application of a five-day work week for all industries, and the encouragement for all individual workers to take more time off from their annual leave days with pay, and so forth (see Figure 8.2).

FIGURE 8.2. Average Number of Authorized Paid Vacation Days per Year, Vacation Days Actually Taken, and Rate of Vacation Utilization (per worker)

Year	Company scale	Authorized vacation days	Vacation days actually taken	Rate of vacation utilization (%)
1980		14.4	8.8	61.3
1985		15.2	7.8	51.6
1990		15.5	8.2	52.9
1991		15.7	8.6	54.6
	1000 employees or more	17.6	10.3	58.3
	100-999	14.9	7.8	52.2
	30-999	13.6	6.9	50.3

Notes: Granted paid vacation days exclude granted paid vacation days carried over to the next fiscal year.
Acquisition rate for granted paid vacation days is no. of acquisition days/no. of granted days.

Source: Nippon, 1993 Business Facts & Figures, JETRO

Yet, the transition may be more difficult in the "walking" than in the "talking." Whereas some workers are in for the idea of working shorter work hours and having more leisure time, others insist on working long, if not longer, for various reasons, including that of getting as much extra income as they used to. Companies–and unions as well–are supportive of the shorter work hour proposition in principle, but when it comes to the matter of actually stopping production lines, paying extra premiums for overtime worked, etc., they appear to be reluctant. To make the story further complicated, in many workplaces, workers feel under pressure psychologically if they go home at the end of the day when others, including their peers, are working hard, especially in some team effort situations.

These cultural factors–mind for group harmony, team work, etc.–tend to deter individual workers from taking as much time off as they would like to. This makes it difficult to reduce the individual's working hours and ultimately the total working hours of all employees in an organization over a year's time. The following table represents the results of a survey made by the Japanese Prime Minister's Office in 1989.

Japanese Workers' Thoughts on Income Versus Free Time

	Male	Female	Total
Want to get more income even if it means my free time may be reduced	26.4%	20.9%	23.4%
Will prefer getting no increase in income to sacrificing my free time	50.9%	53.9%	52.6%
Undecided	19.1%	18.8%	19.0%
Have no idea	3.5%	6.3%	5.1%

The Japanese, without doubt, will continue to look for ways to eventually achieve shorter working hours, but the chances are it will take a long process of "trial and error." Japanese organizations in particular will have to learn one thing, and that is to rid themselves of the traditional custom of depending too heavily on manpower and instead redesign systems and organizations that will require much less labor input; in short, to materialize a "one-man bus," as the Japanese call it. It would be a shame if companies were to continue to leave such systems undone, by merely loading workers with time-consuming work and not paying enough for the time actually spent.

As an example of the Japanese practice of building systems on the premise that abundant labor is available, one Japanese banker points out that almost every Japanese bank has a separate office just for the bank's research or investigation, whereas in other countries the same kind of office is only found in large banks, and that the reason for having such an office is primarily for the staff training and education or job rotation.

Recently Japanese newspapers and magazines have been reporting that: (1) some employers fail to pay workers overtime allowances of any type; (2) employees working overtime are not getting paid for the extra work they have done; and (3) some workers even complete their work at home, again for no reimbursement whatsoever from the employer.

REFERENCE NOTES

1. Volvo, Sanford C. Bernstein, Krafcik/M.I.T., 1993. *The New York Times.*
2. Shuji Hayashi, 1984. *Keiei to Bunka (Culture and Management in Japan).* Tokyo: Chuo Koron Sha. Also in Shuji Hayashi, *Culture and Management in Japan.* Translation by Frank Baldwin, Tokyo: University of Tokyo Press, 1988.

Chapter 9

Conclusion

In bringing this book to a close, it seems appropriate to put all the eight values together in one place and see how they may relate to each other and, particularly, how they are being affected by the changes that are taking place in Japan today, or are likely to take place in the near future.

Japan is now facing dramatic changes in the workforce demography. Some of the more striking of these are (1) a declining birthrate, (2) an aging population, and (3) a resulting chronic shortage of labor. The declining birthrate is bound to accelerate the aging society, which in turn will cause the decline in family savings. Field data released by the Welfare Ministry show that the three population indicators–"productive age population" (those in the age bracket between 15 and 64 years), "silvering age population" (those in the 65 years and over age bracket), and "young age population" (under 15 years old)–together point to the decline in the country's population, particularly the working population, in the coming years (see Figure 9.1). In fact, the Welfare Ministry of the Japanese Government estimates that after the peak year of 1995, Japan's working population will decline by ten million within twenty years.

In the meantime, and as a matter of more immediate concern, Japanese industrial companies are now facing the challenge of restructuring and downsizing because of recessionary pressures. This means that Japanese management now has two separate issues to solve at the same time. One, on a long-term basis, they must plan to secure or maintain needed manpower by investing more in mechanization and other labor-saving devices or by introducing more systems where women, non-Japanese, and senior citizens are more readily accepted into the workforce. Two, as a short-term goal, Japanese managers have to find ways to streamline their organizations to become more cost competitive in an increasingly tight market. Already companies have started announcing plans to get rid of their extra staff (mostly middle aged and elderly) by means of "early retirement" and other programs.

An aging workforce and an increasing number of female workers are by no means new to Japanese, as illustrated in Figures 9.2 and 9.3. Yet, with the downturn of the economy, Japanese companies are now facing challenges they have never experienced before, including pressure to seriously consider using as yet untapped labor

FIGURE 9.1. Projected Population by Age Category

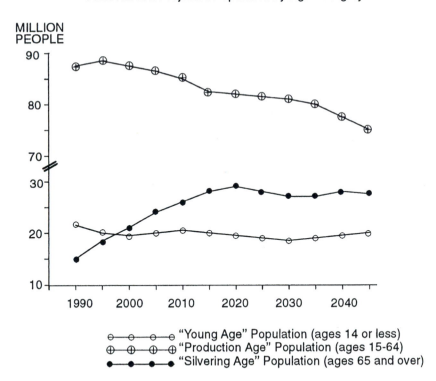

Source: Welfare Ministry, Japanese Government

FIGURE 9.2. Aging Workforce (55 Years of Age and Older) as Percentage of Total Workforce

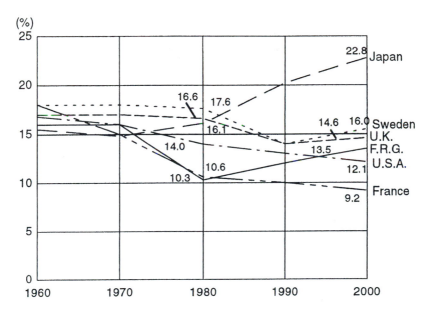

Source: *Management 21*, June 1991 (Original source: ILO Economically Active Population, Estimates and Projections [1985])

resources such as women, retired workers, and foreign-born workers.

But, more important perhaps, Japanese companies will have to learn, among other things, the need to get things done more systematically in the workplace. In the past, both management and labor have tended to seek solutions to problems primarily by throwing in a great number of people or time. Apparently, such "luxurious days" are gone. Because of a shrinking workforce and the need to tighten their belts, companies are now being forced to shift emphasis from a reliance on abundant manpower, or human capital, to emphasis on creating a more efficient workforce, or "information capital," or the introduction of the "one-man bus," as it is called in Japan.

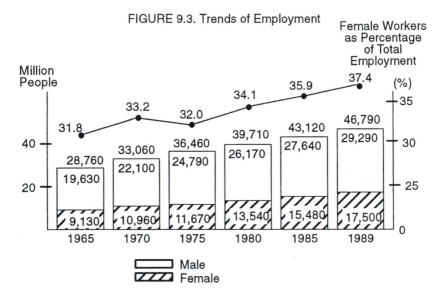

FIGURE 9.3. Trends of Employment

Source: *Management 21*, June 1991 (Original source: Survey of Labor Force by Bureau of General Affairs, Japanese Government)

In addition, management will have to take into consideration various value changes that are taking place in the minds of people they manage. For example, mid-career recruitment will become a thing of common occurrence in the near future, and more and more workers will gladly change workplaces in pursuit of jobs that may be more challenging, rewarding, or less stressful–and from a relatively short-term perspective at that.

Companies will have to be aware of other value changes that are either in progress or are likely to take place. Such changes have already been discussed in relation to the eight value orientations in Japanese business practice. But in conclusion, I would like to review these major changes taking place in Japan and their implications in a broader perspective.

Group Orientation

The deeply ingrained propensity of the Japanese to be or do things together with others is not likely to change drastically, even though there will be more people who dare to be more individualistic than ever before. In the workplace, workers generally will continue to be the "organization man" (good team member), if not the "company man" (loyal employee), although younger generations will tend to be less group oriented and become more assertive than others whenever such an individualistic behavior is accepted.

Some companies are now modifying their human resource systems to reflect the changing attitudes of workers–shifting away from the traditional practice of seniority-based promotion and compensation, and incorporating new concepts of performance-based salary and bonus payment. Companies will be obliged, too, to devise different systems to sustain employees' strong group unity, loyalty, etc., to reflect different values on the part of workers.

The basic group orientation of the Japanese workers, nonetheless, will persist for years, with the majority continuing to be fond of belonging to or participating in different groups of people for different purposes–study, hobby, sports, leisure, in addition to work-related purposes. All indications point to more frequent moves and job changes as a more mobile lifestyle involving more choice is becoming more accepted.

The strong harmony orientation of the Japanese people–including workers–will stay alive and well, and should not be subject to erosion if they are to work with a different family of workers–more women, elderly workers, foreigners, and mid-term recruits. In fact, the chances are this shift from the "homogeneous" to the "heterogeneous" in the workplace population will possibly prompt them to behave in a context different from the past–less Japanese tradition bound but more cosmopolitan in interpersonal relations, for example.

Diligence

This treasured quality of the Japanese people is not likely to yield to the changes ahead, either. Most will continue to work by the sweat of their brow. It is likely, however, that along with the "work is life" majority, a number of Japanese will pursue a more balanced life, incorporating both enjoyable work and stimulating leisure. Most will expect fair pay for a fair day's–or even a fair hour's–work. This will be a new challenge for old-timer employers who used to enjoy extra time or "service" work volunteered by loyal workers.

On a nationwide basis, the possible decrease in a hard-working population may result in solving some of the existing problems but will possibly create new problems in a social context. For example, the number of people suffering from stressful work may diminish, on one hand, but the tradition of frugality among working families is likely to be affected, on the other. In fact, the saving rate of the average Japanese family of 22 percent (of disposable income) ten years ago is already down to the level of 13 to 14 percent.

Aesthetics

The Japanese as a whole will continue to have the same sense of aesthetics. They will continue to turn out quality goods, clean their machines and workplaces to the nth degree before going home, and offer thorough services to others. There seems little possibility of the Japanese ceasing to admire beauty in these ways.

There are things that may make people–especially those from other countries–feel Japanese aesthetics are fading away. Unfortunately, some Japanese exhibit rude arrogance on crowded trains, throw away cigarette butts on the street, spit on the subway stairs, etc. Such reprehensible behavior will continue as an unpleasant habit of carefree Japanese, especially in public or among strangers.

If any real change is occurring in the Japanese aesthetics, it is in the sense of "work versus time" in some workers. Office workers, especially, are already finding less value in staying in their offices after five o'clock to finish a task at hand. They would rather go home, or somewhere else, and do what they like. "Work is work; time is time," they will say.

Love of doing things thoroughly to completion will continue to be an important feature of the Japanese workmanship. This perfectionism, uneconomical as it may seem due to the amount of time it takes to achieve, and unpopular as it may become because it requires intensive devotion, is still likely to be passed down to many Japanese for generations to come.

Curiosity and Emphasis on Innovation

As has been the case, the Japanese will continue to exhibit a strong sense of curiosity in just about every aspect of life that may be different from their own—be it philosophy, religion, politics, economy, technology, culture, or social matters. To Japanese, things "foreign" are and will always be clues to change. They love change because it often promotes creativity and progress. New things are better than old ones.

At the corporate level, the focus on productivity and quality will continue to be a major part of management concern. In particular, Japanese companies' conventional strategic thrust—cost reduction—is likely to continue, and so are suggestion systems and small group activities so long as they contribute to management cost-cutting objectives.

"Kaizen," meaning "betterment" or "continuous improvement," one of the watchwords in Japanese industry, is not likely to weaken in the years ahead.

Respect for Form and Hana Yori Dango

Both in their social lives and in the business world, the Japanese people will no doubt continue to inherit and respect established forms or patterns. Such conformity to, or observance of, social forms, ceremonies, and other patterns are likely to persist so long as people derive some feelings of comfort, or beauty, or efficiency out of doing so. Some Japanese, including businesspeople, even consider that having certain solemn rituals as part of their lives is critical for personal discipline. "Morning sessions," as practiced by a number of Japanese factories each morning, are just one such example.

In the meantime, the Japanese are apt to continue aspiring for "dumplings before flowers." More and more Japanese are, in fact, becoming pragmatic. For example, there are reportedly some salaried workers who show interest only in those activities that will have a direct bearing on their promotion in rank with the company, e.g., going golfing with their bosses over weekends, etc.

Organizations will not be beaten by individuals when it comes to the matter of self-interest. Some, for example, are extremely sensitive to possible infringement by outsiders upon their vested interests. Reported in the newspapers from time to time are the incidents of a group of small shops comprising certain shopping centers bonding together to keep newcomers from operating in the neighborhood, a practice which even keeps influential department stores from opening a new branch store in their shopping districts. Obviously such pragmatists are on the increase.

A Mind for Competition and Outlook on Rewards

The Japanese propensity for competing with others will remain unchanged. They will continue to believe that in the long run free competition will be good for business and for the society at large.

At the corporate level, Japanese inter-company competition can occasionally "overheat" because of such cultural factors as "face-saving," and during times of slow economic growth it can result in so-called "excessive competition." On the other hand, there are those businesspersons who become harsher, if not more disdainful, if companies start competing on the basis of a focus on certain unfair conducts, and even sometimes pursue individual, self-serving goals.

In effect, many Japanese will continue to either approve or disapprove of competition depending on whether it remains within the borders of ethical and moral property. Generally, people will support competition–and business activity in general–if they see in it some contribution to job creation and other social benefits over pure profit-making propositions.

Japanese opinions on rewards and money will also continue to be diverse. On one hand, a greater value will be placed on material compensation in general, but at the same time people are likely to weigh such non-monetary rewards as fame, trust, and incentive for living just as heavily. The money earned by hard work will be the "money with value," while that which comes effortlessly, like a gift from a sibling, the "money without worth."

Silence as Eloquence

Gone are the days when people admired silence. With the Japanese society becoming increasingly internationalized, chances are

good that people will weigh the individual's ability to speak elo-
quently and to be assertive, to be candid, open, and straightforward
much more than before; no more "silence is golden," or "the
mouth is a source of trouble." And no more three Ss–sleeping,
smiling, and silence–of Japanese participants at international meetings.

Already, in the business world and elsewhere in Japanese society,
a small trend is starting toward appreciating eloquence as a preferable style of communication, especially in an international context.
Businesspeople are learning that they will continue to face such
challenges in the area of international communication as:

- The need to become more outspoken and expressive, and to
  avoid relying on contextual inference or "mind-reading,"
- The need to apply more theoretical or deductive reasoning,
- The need to recognize the importance of written communication in an international setting, and
- The need to cultivate more skilled international "communicators" among Japanese.

Perception of Time

In spite of the fact that the Japanese people are relatively impa-
tient, punctual, and sensitive about meeting deadlines such as delivery dates, many still tend to take time in getting things done. In the
minds of the Japanese, time is often secondary to other values–easily disposable if the circumstances so dictate. Many, for example,
will willingly spend time, and tend to expect others to do the same,
whenever there seems to be a need for better communication, stronger human relations (including building of trust), respect for others'
formalities, or simply to be in tune with others' pace, etc. The idea
of "make haste slowly" often overrides any sense of wasting time.

At the corporate level, however, this tradition of accomplishing
things through extensive use of time–or almost abuse of time–is
likely to become a target of serious reflection and criticism. On one
hand, management is and will continue to be under pressure to
improve the productivity of its workforce in terms of per hour
output (rather than per day output) in order to become even more
competitive. Both management and labor will have to find ways to

get their work done faster and in less time, to become more time efficient, not only on production floors, where efficiency is already very high, especially in mass production industries, but in other staff offices as well.

On the other hand, pressures are mounting to reduce the working hours of Japanese workers, both from outside Japan and from within. On average, Japanese workers are working at least several hundred hours more annually than their counterparts in other industrialized countries–a source of harsh remarks from outside–and these extra hours reportedly are the result of irregular work habits more or less forced on workers, such as excessive overtime, intimidation of use of one's accrued leave time or paid holidays, and the like–which is a source of discontent from within Japan.

So the next few years will witness a number of companies making efforts to narrow the gap between the Western work hour averages and those of Japan, to provide greater benefits to their workers, such as reduced work hours. However, it appears that the target of 1,800 work hours per year, set by the Japanese government, will not be achieved in the foreseeable future. Some companies are, in fact, already against the idea of shortening the work hours at the sacrifice of productivity, and chances are many more will follow suit. Here, again, some Japanese are likely to "take time" to achieve national goals of importance to them.

The Japanese long-term orientation will continue to be a major part of corporate planning such as capital investment, marketing, human resources training, and development. The Japanese will most likely continue to believe in the benefit of a long-term view over that of short-term considerations.

Last, because of its relevance to Japanese business values in general, mention should be made briefly of the changing attitudes of Japanese women vis-à-vis work versus home, and of the work ethic of young Japanese in general.

First, Japanese women are placing greater value on working outside of the home than ever before. Statistic show that in 1992, 19.3 million women (a little over 40 percent of the total labor force) were working–an unprecedented number in Japan's history.

Noteworthy in recent years has been the trend of housewives joining the workforce on a part-time basis. Much like the United

States in the 1970s, gone are the days when it was considered a good custom for a married woman to stay at home. Now working outside the home is a well-accepted change.

One of the old stereotypical notions of the Japanese women quitting work upon getting married or having children is now changing. A survey conducted by a private research organization in 1992 revealed that of 250 unmarried women, those who said they "will quit working upon marriage" numbered 27 percent, those who "will quit working upon childbirth" were 28 percent, and those who "will not quit working either upon marriage or childbirth" were 24 percent–close to an even split between the three alternatives. Add to this another 20 percent who said they "will stay single," and the result is obvious: Japanese women's values are becoming diverse on the matter of work versus home life. In another survey, 20.5 percent (or roughly one-fifth of unmarried women surveyed) indicated that they would quit work upon marriage and childbirth, while 12.7 percent said they would work as long as possible. Fifty-eight percent indicated it was best for a woman to work for one company and then take another job after temporary leave for marriage and childbirth.[1]

Reflecting one of the growing trends among female workers in Japan are terms such as "career woman" and "quasi-career woman." The "career woman" is equivalent to that which is prevalent in the U.S. and elsewhere–referring to a competent professional woman, usually with a university degree, who seeks to pursue a specific career in a professional field. In Japan, if a woman chooses to pursue such a career goal, companies will now consider hiring her as a candidate for some "sogoshoku" (career track job) as against "ippanshoku" (general office work). These two job categories have been established in Japanese companies for some years now as a result of stricter enforcement of the Japanese Equal Employment Opportunity Law.

Reports are, however, that despite this development, in actual reality there are not yet very many career women, with the majority of women workers preferring to pursue a quasi-career to a career. Why? They are loath to be involved in a world of harsh competition, and are usually less flexible regarding geographic transfers. Because they are generally perfectionists and hard workers, they would rather value their personal life over work. Comments one human resource manager at NEC, a corporation which hires more than 200 women graduates per year, "In short, they on average lack an upwardly mobile mentality; they display too little robustness or sturdiness to be called career women. This is certainly a large part of why women as yet constitute just one percent of all managerial positions in Japan."

As the economy slows down, chances are that Japanese women's career orientation–as far as long-term employment with the same company, at least–may further shrink. Instead, we may see an increase in quasi-career women.

In relation to the Equal Employment Opportunity Law that went into effect in 1986, while it was considered to be a boost to place more and more career track women into the workforce, in 1991 only 3.6 percent of women workers in companies with more than 100 employees held middle management positions up to the level of section chief, according to the Ministry of Labor.[3]

Second, there are indications that the attitudes of young Japanese toward work is changing. One such indication was reflected in the result of a recent survey which showed that in selecting a place of work, the average Japanese was choosing a job mainly on the basis of the type of work, rather than on the basis of a big company name or image, which used to be the case with the Japanese years ago. In fact, there are even signs that suggest that young Japanese are becoming more in favor of working for foreign affiliated corporations or joint venture companies instead of big domestic enterprises.

Another survey made of newly hired young employees in Japanese companies revealed that a good number of them–50 percent of male and 60 percent of female workers surveyed–had some feeling of dissatisfaction with the work they were doing, and would like to change jobs. Unlike their predecessors, the young are insisting on pursuing a lifestyle which bases self-satisfaction less on work and more on personal time. This trend has been persisting after the so-called baby-boomer generation.

Also reflecting the young workers' changing attitudes is their tendency to "call it a day" or take a leave of absence whenever they like, with much less hesitance than their senior colleagues would or used to have. The Japanese media once labeled such young Japanese a "new breed," and now the "new breed" is often referred to as being fond of three K's–"kankyo" (environmental influence), "kaiteki" (comfortable condition), and "kyuka" (vacations). Boye De Mente, a Japan specialist, writes: ". . . their attitude is that they do not want to work for companies unless they are environmentally responsible, provide comfortable working conditions, and encourage their employees to take vacations."[3]

It is difficult to believe, however, that the "new breed" will remain new forever. True, young people are softening in many ways–they are more individualistic, more self-serving, more demanding, more pragmatic–often enough to concern older generations. Yet the general impression and consensus among Japanese business managers is that, once young people become members of a large organization and are immersed in its pool of disciplines, they will learn to appreciate the traditional values of their elders and that most, if not all, of them go on to a work life just as group oriented, hardworking, loyal, competition minded, and tradition bound as preceding generations.

Pressure for social change, both from within Japan and from without, will no doubt influence Japanese social life and values in the long run. Yet cultural values and beliefs at the heart of Japanese business practice discussed here have a long history and are deeply ingrained. As an old Japanese proverb states, a deep river runs slowly.

REFERENCE NOTES

1. The Prime Minister's Office survey of worker consciousness, 1992.

2. Focus Japan, JETRO, July/August, 1993.

3. Boye DeMente, 1992. "The Three Ks and the Tribal Test." *The Journal of the American Chamber of Commerce in Japan,* October. Tokyo: ACCJ.

Bibliography

The year in parenthesis is that of the first publication of the work in any language; the second year is that of the source used.

Abegglen, James C. 1958. *The Japanese Factory: Aspects of Its Social Organization.* New York: The Free Press.

Abegglen, James C. and Stalk, George, Jr. 1986. Translation: *Ueyama, Shuichiro. Kaisha (The Japanese Corporation).* Tokyo: Kodansha.

Adams, T.F.M. and Kobayashi, N. (1969) 1974. *The World of Japanese Business.* Tokyo: Kodansha International.

Asahi Shimbun Gaihobu, ed. 1986. *Soto kara Mita Nippon (Japan as Seen from Abroad).* Tokyo: Asahi Shimbun.

Ballon, Robert J. 1982. Minutes of Ichigukai Seminar: Aoi Me de Mita Nihonteki Keiei (Japanese style management as seen from blue eyes). Tokyo: Japan Management Association Ichigukai.

Barnland, Dean C. 1979. Translation: *Nishiyama, Sen and Sano, Masako. Nihonjin no Hyogen Hozo. (Public and Private Self in Japan and the United States).* Tokyo: Simul Press.

Benedict, Ruth. (1946) 1974. *The Chrysanthemum and the Sword.* Tokyo: Charles E. Tuttle Company.

A Bilingual Guide. 1985. *Japan As It Is.* Tokyo: Gakken.

Bowles, Jerry. April 1992. Is American Management Really Committed to Quality? *AMA Management Reviews.*

Bresinski, Zbigniew. (1972). Translation: *Otsuki, Jin-ichi. Hiyowana Hana Nippon (The Fragile Blossom–Crisis and Change in Japan)* 1977. Tokyo: Simul Press.

Buckley, Roger. 1985. *Japan Today.* Cambridge: Cambridge University Press.

Chio, Masaru. July 1, 1978. *Is Japanese Distribution System Really So Complicated?* Japan Management Association Newsletter. Tokyo: JMA.

The Chosun Ilbo, ed. 1984. *Kankokujin ga Mita Nippon (Japan as Seen by Koreans)*. Tokyo: Simul Press.

Christopher, Robert C. 1983. *The Japanese Mind*. Tokyo: Kodansha.

Clark, Gregory. 1977. Translation: *Muramatsu, Masumi. Nipponjin: Yunikusa no Gensen (The Japanese Tribe: Origins of a Nation's Uniqueness)*. Tokyo: Simul Press.

Condon, John C., Jr. 1980. Translation: Kondo, Chie. *Ibunkakan communication (Cultural Dimentions of Communication)*. Tokyo: Simul Press.

De Mente, Boye. 1981. *Japanese Manners & Ethics in Business.* Phoenix: Phoenix Books.

De Mente, Boye. 1986. Translation: *Hasuda, Toshifumi and Amakawa, Yukiko. Nihonka suru America (The Japanization of America)*. Tokyo: Chukei Shuppan.

Dertouzos, Michael L., Lester, Richard K., Solow, Robert M. Translation: Yodá, Nooya. 1990. *Made in America.* Tokyo: Soushisha.

The Dimension Research Seminar, ed. 1989. New Theories of Creative Management (Sozosuru Soshiki no Kenkyuu). Tokyo: Kodansha.

Doi, Takeo. (1973) 1986. *The Anatomy of Dependence.* Tokyo: Kodansha International.

Drucker, P. F. 1971. What Can We Learn From Japanese Management? *Harvard Business Review*, March.

Fields, George. 1983. *From Bonsai to Levi's–When West Meets East: An Insider's Surprising Account of How Japanese Live.* Macmillan.

Fukuda, Ryukji. 1983. *Managerial Engineering.* Stanford, CN: Productivity Inc.

Fukui, Ken-ichi. 1985. Nihonjin to Dokusosei (The Japanese and Originality) in *Nihon Rashisa (Japanese Essences)*. Tokyo: Kodansha.

Gibney, Frank. 1975. Translation: Omae, Masaomi. *Hito wa Shiro, Hito wa Ishigaki (Japan, the Fragile Superpower)*. Tokyo: Simul Press.

Gow, Ian; Handy, Charles; Gordon, Colin; and Randlesome, Collin. 1989. *Making Managers; 2. Japan.* London: Pitman Publishing.

Harvard Business School Bulletin. "Sunao" (Matsushita)

Hatakeyama, Yoshio. 1985. *Manager Revolution: A Guide to Survival in Today's Changing Workplace.* Stanford, CN: Productivity Press.

Hayashi, Shuji. 1984. *Keiei to Bunka (Culture and Management in Japan).* Tokyo: Chuo Koron Sha.

Hayashi, Shuji. 1988. Translation: Baldwin, Frank. *Culture and Management in Japan.* Tokyo: University of Tokyo Press.

Higuchi, Kotaro. 1991. *Japan Management Association Management News,* May. Tokyo. JMA.

Hollerman, Leon. 1988. Translation: Masudo, Kinya. *Nihon Kabushikikaisha no Hokai (Japan, Disincorporated).* Tokyo: Sanno Daigaku Shuppanbu.

A Hundred More Things Japanese. 1980. Tokyo: Japan Culture Institute.

A Hundred Things Japanese. (1975) 1978. Tokyo: Japan Culture Institute.

Ibuka, Masaru. 1991. *Waga Tomo Honda Soichiro (My Friend, Soichiro Honda).* Tokyo: Goma Shobo

Imai, Masaaki. 1986. *Kaizen.* New York: Random House.

Imai, Masaaki. 1988. *Kaizen (Improvement).* Tokyo: Kobunsha.

International Management Association of Japan, ed. 1989. *Nihon no Keiei no Kokusaisei (Internationalization of Japanese Management).* Tokyo: IMAJ.

Ishikawa, Kaoru. 1974. Guide to Quality Control. Tokyo: Asian Productivity Organization.

Ishikawa, Yoshimi. 1969a. *JMA Management Bulletin,* No. 3. Japanese Type Management and American Type Management. Tokyo: JMA.

Ishikawa, Yoshimi. 1969b. *JMA Management Bulletin,* No. 7. The Zero Defects Movement Is Taking Roots in Japanese Industry. Tokyo: JMA.

Ito, Francisco S. 1989. *Nambei kara Mita Nipponjin (Japanese as Seen from Latin America–What an Emigrant from Brazil Expects of Japan).* Tokyo: Simul Press.

Japan Management Association, ed. 1991. Fact-Finding Survey of Management Issues–1991. Tokyo: JMA.

Japan Management Association, ed. 1985. Japanese Business: Its Environment and Structure. Tokyo: JMA.

Japan Management Association, ed. 1982. International Conference on Productivity and Quality–Conference Minutes. Tokyo: JMA.

JMA Newsletter, Japan Management Association.

The Journal of the American Chamber of Commerce in Japan, July 1991.

Kameda, Hideyuki. 1991. *The Challenge of the Japanese Market: The Manufacturing Success–Nine Foreign Affiliation Companies with Plants in Japan.* Tokyo: JETRO.

Kanayama, Norio. 1979. The Japanese Businessman and His Style of Communication. *JMA Newsletter,* May 1. Tokyo: JMA.

Kanayama, Norio. 1989. *Nippon to Chugoku–Doko ga Chigauka (Japan and Republic of China–Where Are the Differences?).* Tokyo: Nippon Jitsugyo Shuppan Sha.

Kato, Kyoko and Berger, Michael. 1987. *Nipponjin o Shiranai Americajin, Amiricajin o Shiranai Nipponjin (Americans Who Do not Know Japanese and Japanese Who Do not Know Americans).* Tokyo: TBS Britannica.

Keidanren, Geppo, October 1989. *Waga Sha no Shaze Shokun (Our Company Precepts/Principles).* Tokyo: Keidanren.

Keiei Kadai (Fact-Finding Survey of Management Issues). 1991, 1992, 1993. Tokyo: Japan Management Association.

Kigyo, Hakusho. 1986. White Paper on Corporations. Tokyo: Keizai Doyukai.

Kitagawa, Chuichi. 1983. *Nipponjin wo Kangaeru (In Consideration of the Japanese).* Tokyo: Nippon Housou Publishing Association.

Kumazawa, Makoto. 1989. *Nihonteki Keiei no Meian (Japanese Management–Its Bright Side and Dark Side).* Tokyo: Tsukuma Shobo.

Lappe, Frances Moore. 1989. *Rediscovering America's Values.* New York: Ballantine Books.

Lee Do Hyong. 1984. *Kankokujin ga Mita Nippon (Japan as Seen by Koreans).* Tokyo: Simul Press.

Lee Kun. 1984. *Kankokujin ga Mita Nippon (Japan as Seen by Koreans).* Tokyo: Simul Press.

Loke, Pooi-Choon. 1986. Translation: *Hanano, Toshihiko. Hoshoku Nippon–Tounan Ajiya wa Nippon ni Manaberuka (A Land of*

Gluttony: Can Southeast Asia "Look East"?) Tokyo: Simul Press.

March, Robert M. 1988. *The Japanese Negotiator.* Tokyo: Kodansha International.

Maruyama, Yoshinari. 1989. *Nihonteki Keiei–Sono Hozo to Biheibiya (Japanese Management–Its Structures and Behaviors).* Tokyo: Nippon Hyoron Sha.

Matsushita, Konosuke. 1989. *As I See It,* 5th ed. Kyoto: PHP Institute.

Matsushita, Konosuke. 1986. *Han'ei no Tameno Kangaekata (Thoughts on Prosperity).* Kyoto: PHP Institute.

Ministry of International Trade and Industry, ed. 1989. *Nichibei no Kigyo Koudou Hikaku (Comparative Study of Industrial Behaviors Between the United States and Japan).* Tokyo: JMA.

Ministry of Labor, ed. 1993. White Paper on Labor. Tokyo: Nippon Rodo Kenkyu Kiko.

Mitsubishi Motors Corporation Human Resources Department, ed. 1987. *Nippon no Subete (Introduction to Japan).* Tokyo: Sanseido.

Mitsubishi Research Institute, ed. 1990. A Comparative Research on the Activities of Japanese, American, and European Companies. Tokyo.

Miyamoto, Michiko and Nagasawa, Makoto. (1982) 1988. *Amerikajin no Nihonjinkan (Americans Views of Japanese).* Tokyo: Sovshisha.

Moran, Robert T. 1985. *Getting Your Yen's Worth–How to Negotiate with Japan, Inc.* Houston: Gulf Publishing Company.

Morita, Akio. 1992. *Nihonteki Keiei ga Abunai (Japanese Management in a Crisis).* Bungei-Shunju, February. Tokyo.

Morita, Akio and Ishihara, Shintaro. (1989) 1990. *"No" to Ieru Nippon (The Japan that Can Say "No").* Tokyo: Kobunsha.

Morita, Akio, Shimomura, Mitsuko and Rheingold, E. 1990. *Made in Japan.* Tokyo: Asahi Shimbunsha.

Moritani, Masanori. 1982. *Japanese Technology.* Tokyo: Simul Press.

Nakajima, Mineo. 1990. *Nipponjin to Chugokujin Kokoga Ochigai (The Major Differences Between the Japanese and Chinese).* Tokyo: Nesuko.

Nakajima, Takayoshi. 1990. *Consulting no Rutsu o Saguru (Probing the Roots of JMAC Consulting)*. Tokyo: JMA Consultants, Inc.

Nakane, Chie. 1970. *Japanese Society*. Berkeley: University of California Press.

Nakatani, Iwao. *Will*, May 1989.

The New York Times, 1993. Volvo, Sanford C., Bernstein, Krafcik/ M.I.T.

Nihon Mirai Gakkai, ed. 1989. *Nippongo wa Kokusaigo ni Naruka (Will the Japanese Language Become an International Language?)*. Tokyo: TBS Britanica.

Nippon. 1993. JETRO. Business Facts and Figures.

Nippon Keizai Shimbun, ed. 1989. *Terasu de Yomu Nihon no Keiei (Japanese Management to Be Studied on Terrace)*. Tokyo: Keizai Shimbunsha.

Nippon Keizai Shimbun. 1992. How Different Are Japanese and American Corporate Management? November, 1992.

Nippon Steel Corporation, ed. 1987. *Nihon no Kororo (Essays on Japan from Japan)*. Tokyo: Maruzen.

Nippon Research Center. 1992. Market Yoken (Market Projections): From Euphoria Syndrome to a Sane Society. December.

Nishibori, Eizaburo. 1985. Nihonjin wa Naze Yoku Hatarakuka (Why the Japanese Work so Hard?) in *Nihon Rashisa (Japanese Essences)*. Tokyo: Kodansha.

Nishikawa, Shunsaku, ed. 1980. *The Labor Market in Japan*. Tokyo: University of Tokyo Press.

Nishiyama, Sen. 1991. *Shin Gokai to Rikai (Understanding and Misunderstanding, new ed.)*. Tokyo: Simul Press.

Nishizawa, Jun-ichi. 1989. *Gijutsu Taikoku Nihon no Mirai o Yomu (A Look into the Future of Japan–The Technological Superpower)*. Kyoto: PHP Institute.

Odaka, Kunio. 1988. *Nihonteki Keiei (Japanese-Style Management)*. Tokyo: Chuokoronsha.

Ogawa, Kazuhisa, Sasaki, Yoshiaki and Kawase, Suguru. 1988. *Kijakusei: Nippon wa Ikinokoreruka (Fragility–Can the Japanese Survive?)*. Tokyo: Yoyosha.

Ogawa, Morimasa. 1991. *Pana Management*. Kyoto: PHP Institute.

Okumura, Hiroshi. 1979. Corporate Capitalism in Japan–Japanese

Companies and Management, *JMA Newsletter,* February. Tokyo: JMA.

Osada, Takashi. 1991. *The 5S–Five Keys to a Total Quality Environment.* Tokyo: Asian Productivity Organization.

Passin, Herbert. 1982. *Society and Education in Japan.* Tokyo: Kodansha International.

Perin, Constance. 1988. *Belonging in America: Reading Between the Lines.* Wisconsin: The University of Wisconsin Press.

Rebischung, James. 1973. *Japan: The Facts of Modern Business and Social Life.* Tokyo: Charles E. Tuttle Company.

Reischauer, Edwin O. (1977) 1983. *The Japanese.* Tokyo: Charles E. Tuttle Company.

Reischauer, Edwin O. (1970) 1981. *Japan: The Story of a Nation.* Tokyo: Charles E. Tuttle Company.

Reischauer, Edwin O. (1977) 1979. Translation: Kunihiro, Masao. *The Japanese.* Tokyo: Bungei Shunju.

Rokeach, Milton. 1973. *The Nature of Human Values.* New York: The Free Press.

Sabata, Toyoyuki. 1985. Komezukuri ni Nezashita Nihon no Bunka (The Rice Cultivation Oriented Culture of Japan), in *Nihon Bunka o Saguru (Behind Japanese Culture).* Tokyo: Kodansha.

Sagara, Toru. 1980. *Seijitsu to Nipponjin (Sincerity and the Japanese).* Tokyo: Perikansha.

Sakakibara, Kiyonori. (1989) 1990. *Jinzai no Joken (Conditions for Human Resources).* Kyoto: PHP Institute.

Sakamoto, Shigeyasu. 1990. *Hontoni Nippon no Seisansei wa Takainoka (Is the Japanese Productivity Truly so High?).* Tokyo: JMA.

Sataka, Makoto. 1991. Tosei Kigyo *Annai (Guide to Present Day Industry).*

Sato, Sadaharu. 1992. *Gekidou ni Ikiru Keieisha Kanrisha (Executives and Managers Who Survive in Times of Turbulence).* Fukuoka: Shudan-Rikigaku Kenkyusho.

Shiba, Ryotaro. 1990. *Kono Kuni no Katachi 1 and 2 (The Shape of this Country: 1 and 2).* Tokyo: Bungei Shunju.

Shiba, Ryotaro. (1978) 1990. *Taidanshu: Nipponjin wo Kangaeru (Considering the Japanese People).* Tokyo: Bungei Shunju.

Shiba, Ryotaro. (1981) 1990. *Taidanshu; Rekishi wo Kangaeru (Considering the Japanese History).* Tokyo: Bungei Shunju.

Shimizu, Ryuei. 1986. *Top Management in Japanese Firms.* Tokyo: Chikura Shobo.

Sitaram, K. S. 1985. Translation: Midooka, Kiyoshi. *Ibunka kan Communication (Foundations of Intercultural Communication).* Tokyo: Tokyo Sogen Sha.

Steward, Jack and Van Zandt, Howard. 1985. Japan: *The Hungry Guest.* Tokyo: Lotus Press.

Suzuki, Takao, Nitoda, Rokusaburo and Kawakami, Masamitsu. 1983. *Nipponjin: Sono Gengo, Shukyo, and Dokusosei (The Japanese: Their Language, Religion, and Originality).* Tokyo: JMA.

Suzumura, Kikuo. 1984. Mass Production is Out of Step with the Times. *JMA Newsletter,* No. 19.

Takeuchi, Hitoshi. 1990. *Daihyoteki Nipponjin (Representative Japanese).* Tokyo: Dobun Shoin.

Takezawa, Shin-ichi. 1979. Changing Worker Values and Management Innovations in Japanese Industry. *Labour and Society,* Vol. 4, No. 2.

Tanikawa, Tetsuzo. 1988. N*ipponjin no Kokoro (The Japanese Mind).* Tokyo: Kodansha.

Taylor, Jared. 1984. *Shadows of the Rising Sun.* Tokyo: Kobunsha.

Tokyo Business Today. March 1992. Morita Shock: New Paradigm Needed for Japanese Management.

Totoki, Akira. 1974. *People Who Make Companies and Companies That Make People.* Tokyo: JMA.

Totoki, Akira. 1977. *Productivity Improvement in Japan: A Nationwide Case Study.* Tokyo: JMA.

Toyota, Aritsune. 1990. *Nipponjin to Kankokujin Kokoga Ochigai (The Major Differences Between the Japanese and Koreans).* Tokyo: Nesuko.

Tsuchiya, Moriaki. (1974) 1989. *Harvard Business School nite (At the Harvard Business School).* Tokyo: Chuo Koronsha.

Tsuda, Masumi. 1987. *Nihonteki Keiei wa Dokoe Ikunoka (Japanese Management: Where is it Headed?).* Kyoto: PHP Institute.

Uchihashi, Katsuto. 1991. *Sonkei Okuatawazane Kigyo (Companies Unworthy of Respect).* Tokyo: Kobunsha.

Umesao, Tadao, ed. (1985) 1989. *77 Keys to Japanese Civilization.* Osaka: Sogensha.

Van Zandt, Howard F. 1972. Learning to Do Business with "Japan Inc." *Harvard Business Review,* July-August.

Vogel, Ezra F. 1979. *Japan as Number One–Lessons for America.* Cambridge: Harvard University Press.

Vogel, Ezra F. 1979. Translation: *Hironaka, Wakako, and Kimoto, Akiko. Japan as Number One.* Tokyo: TBS Britanica.

Vogel, Ezra F. (1979) 1985. *Modern Japanese Organization and Decision Making.* Tokyo: Charles E. Tuttle Company.

Whitehill, Arthur M. 1991. *Japanese Management: Traditions and Transition.* London: Routledge.

Yamaki, Naomi. 1980. *Nihon no Manejimento (Japanese Management).* Tokyo: JMA.

Yamamoto, Shichihei. 1989. *Nipponjin towa Nanika (Who Are the Japanese?).* Kyoto: PHP Institute.

Yanagida, Kunio. 1984. *Nippon no Gyakuten Shita Hi (The Day Japan Began to Win).* Tokyo: Kodansha.

Yashiro, Masamoto. 1992. *How Different Are Japanese and American Corporate Management?* Tokyo: Nihon Keizai Shimbunsha.

Yoshihara, Kunio. 1982. *Sogo Shosha–The Vanguard of the Japanese Economy.* Oxford: Oxford University Press.

Zimmerman, Mark. 1985. *How to Do Business with The Japanese–A Strategy for Success.* New York: Random House.

Index

Page numbers in italics indicate figures; page numbers followed by t indicate tables.